I0157195

REVIEWS

A whimsical, unique collection of humorous takes on nursery rhymes, talking horses and chicken-fried steak, among other topics.

It's certainly a short story collection like no other: In one tale, a man named Murray apparently time travels to meet Jesus, who urges him to blog about the experience; Murray later becomes Jesus' speechwriter and falls for Mary Magdalene. Another sketch features two writers discussing the fine art of the short story while completely missing each other's points; still another depicts one man's search for the secret behind chicken-fried steak.

This book's subject matter is as light and fluffy as a slice of chocolate mousse pie, and each story features concise, easily digestible prose. Royce's eclectic collection, including song lyrics about runaway shoes, cleverly captioned cartoons about hot dogs and a short story about the last fateful days of the beloved talking horse Mr. Ed, will likely reward readers with laugher.

A wide-ranging, rollicking good collection of comedic sketches.

Kirkus Reviews

REVIEWS

I met Bill Royce a hundred and fifty years ago when I was going to college in Santa Cruz, California. He was always clever and satirical with an offbeat sense of humor and, without a doubt, smarter than all the wanna-be intellectuals I knew in school.

But a lot can happen in a hundred and fifty years. You live a life, you have a kid, you lose a friend and then your heart gets so full that you do and say silly and beautiful things. This tender-hearted, quirky collection of short stories is sometimes hilarious, sometimes perverted, often twisted, more often total genius, and always silly and beautiful. Filled with puns, double entendres, and witty interpretations, Royce re-invents the stories of old nursery rhymes and other familiar anecdotes. You marvel at his creativity, artistry and his ridiculous imagination.

My old friend Bill Royce is still very clever, funny and offbeat. But he's also an insightful and brilliant writer. The proof is in the pages of this book.

~ Camryn Manheim ~ Actress & Author

I Know Why
the Caged Pig Oinks

And Other Love Stories

Also by WILLIAM JAMES ROYCE

NOVELS

Monkey Island

The Immaculate Deception
A Tom Sullivan Mystery

I Know Why
the Caged Pig Oinks

And Other Love Stories

WILLIAM JAMES ROYCE

This is a work of fiction. Names, characters, places, and incidents are either the product of the author's imagination or are used fictitiously and/or satirically. Any resemblance to actual people, living or dead, locales or events is merely coincidental.

I KNOW WHY THE CAGED PIG OINKS
And Other Love Stories
Copyright © 2012 by William James Royce

Original Artwork © 2012 by William James Royce
All rights reserved.

No portion of this book may be reproduced or transmitted in any form or by any means without written permission from the Publisher.

Chanticleer Publishing
1540 Broadway
New York, NY 10036
www.ChanticleerPublishing.com

First Black & White Paperback Edition: January 2013
10 9 8 7 6 5 4 3 2 1

"Stardust" music by Hoagy Carmichael, lyrics by Mitchell Parish. Copyright © 1929 by Songs of Peer, Ltd. All rights controlled and administered by EMI Mills Music, Inc. Used by kind permission.

All photography unidentified and public domain unless otherwise indicated.

Cover design copyright © 2012 by William James Royce. All rights reserved.

ISBN: 978-0615750439

Printed in the United States of America.

For Jim Whearty

CONTENTS

ONE

TWO

The Last of the Moe Howards

Great Post-Card Art with Sister Mary Fred: Parisian Delight

The Lost Testament: The Gospel According to St. Murray

When Pigs Fly!

"The Collaboration"

The By-Poehler Review with Byron Poehler

"Lost Soles Blues" (Transcript)

Mr. Ed, The Final Days

THREE

The Low Brows

Deleted Bible Stories: Lot's Brother ("The Peanut Man")

Holstein vs. O'Looney, The Great Debate

Great Post-Card Art with Sister Mary Fred: The Donut Queen

"O Brother, Where Aren't Thou?"

Post-Card Rate Theatre

Weenie & Bun

FOUR

ONE

Where Are They Now?

Dish & Spoon

"Where Are They Now?"

The Dish & the Spoon

ANNOUNCER: Tonight, in their own words, the Dish & the Spoon will tell you the real story. The true story. The story your parents never wanted you to hear.

The CAMERA PANS the inside of their filthy doublewide trailer. The DISH stands at the sink, doing the dishes; giving the "little ones" a bath.

The SPOON is kicked back, chocolate ice cream dripping down his handle, ogling a Ginzo Knife commercial on TV.

ANNOUNCER: Although the Dish clearly shows the signs of aging – the chipping and the cracking. Remarkably, the Spoon looks today almost exactly the --

SPOON: (*into Camera*) Well, you know, silverware ages better. It's a known fact.

ANNOUNCER: The Spoon looks almost exactly the same today as he did that fateful day when they infamously ran away together, shocking an entire nation already torn asunder, what with the cat and that incessant fiddle, the damn little dog laughing like a lunatic, and who could ever forget that cow?

SPOON: Anyone who tells you they remember the night the cow jumped over the moon wasn't really there, man.

ANNOUNCER: To fully comprehend their dramatic story, it's imperative that we paint a portrait of this poignant period.

SPOON: What can I say? It was a crazy night. You know, we were young and foolish. I was using dish soap straight back then. We're talking phosphates, baby! The Real Thing.

ANNOUNCER: How did you two actually meet?

SPOON: You know, man, this was back when people actually washed and dried their dishes – by hand! You know, all that static electricity from the drying towel just zipping around the room. Damn, she looked fine in that drying rack, all buffed and lemony fresh. I'll never forget the first time I saw her…

The MUSIC *indicates that we are* DISSOLVING *back in time to a Christmas dinner, long ago. The "good" China has been set, along with the crystal goblets. The Spoon is set beside his buddy, the* KNIFE. *They rest on the fine Irish lace tablecloth.*

KNIFE: Hey --

SPOON (V.O.) He says to me,

KNIFE: -- get a loada the dish beside me!

The Spoon tries to see past him.

SPOON: (V.O.) But I could only get a glimpse of her past that big fat blade of his.

KNIFE: Now's your chance!

SPOON: (V.O.) He says to me, as this pudgy little hand grabs him by the handle and whisks him away. There she was... What a profile! Not a single chip. One look and you could tell this was a dish who'd never been used. I hated to think what would happen to her if we stayed... I'd seen 'em come and go over the years.

DISH: You know, back then it wasn't socially acceptable.

SPOON: People would gawk. Oh yeah, they'd gawk! Openly! Openly gawking! Turns out, openly gawking is specifically reserved for this kinda thing!

ANNOUNCER: (*into Camera*) Of course the lives of the children are the real tragedy in any mixed marriage. The offspring of the Dish and the Spoon are, alas, no exception.

SPOON: Yeah, it hasn't been easy on little Spish.

DISH: Children can be so cruel.

SPOON: I'll never forget, poor little Spish, she comes running home from school one day all in tears. Some kid called her a "doon".

DISH: A *dirty little* doon!

SPOON: Ouch! You know, she'd never heard that word before.

DISH: Then, of course, there are all the questions.

SPOON: Like, Hey Mister, what is she? Metal? Ceramic?

DISH: *Meramic?*

ANNOUNCER: *(into Camera)* Time has not been kind to the Dish and the Spoon. Rumors run rampant; affairs, infidelities, improprieties –

SPOON: Improprieties? I don't know what you heard – she's a half-teaspoon.

ANNOUNCER: Mr. Spoon?

SPOON: …Okay, it's true – she's only a quarter, but she looks twice her size!

ANNOUNCER: *(Into Camera)* Before you feel too sorry for the Dish –

SPOON: That's right! Y'ever try to spoon with a dish? Forget it! It's impossible!

DISH: Let me remind you that I was fine China, not that "bone" China from Ireland that you seem to prefer!

SPOON: Get stacked already!

DISH: *(Into Camera)* I was China. He was silver-plated… cutlery. To me, he was nothing more than a… utensil. A spoon, no less! Not even a soupspoon. Just a regular, plain ol' spoon. Despite what he says, I'd been around the table a time or two. I even flirted with a prominent fork once. And not a salad fork, either.

Dish stares off, lost in thought.

DISH: …I remember his spikes were long, and slightly curved. There he was, upside down, the tips of his spikes resting on my lip, a thin layer of turkey gravy the only thing between us. "Hey," he says to me, "Didn't I see you last Easter?" "Me?" I says, coyly. "Yeah, yeah," he says. "You were covered in ham at the time, and what appeared to be – whoa! – Gotta go!" And with that, he was gone. I heard from a dessert plate that he got bent at a Christmas dinner and rarely gets out of the drawer anymore. Sad…

ANNOUNCER: (*into Camera*) Well, there you have it. The incredibly sad story of the Dish & the Spoon. Where Are They Now? They're a sad footnote in our collective unconscious.

SPOON: (*off-screen*) What the hell are you talkin' about? Collective unconscious – we're right here!

ANNOUNCER: Join us next time, won't you?

DISH: (*off-screen*) What's this about you and a quarter teaspoon?!

SPOON: (*Off-screen*) She looked like a half – easy!

ANNOUNCER: For another episode of Where Are They Now?

Fade to black.

WEENIE & BUN

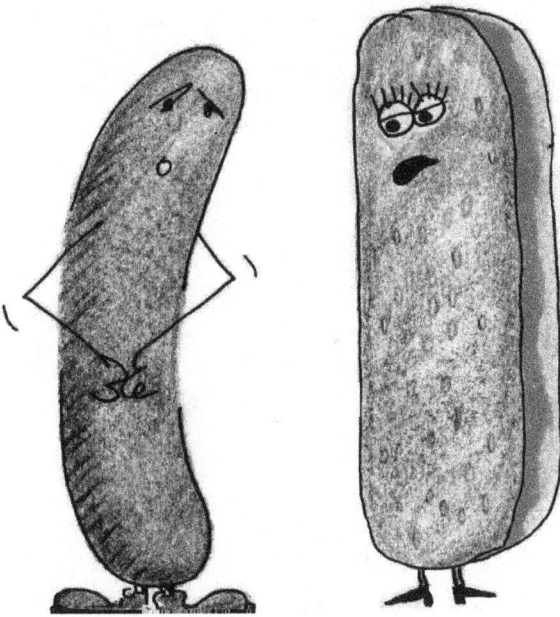

"You know, it does kinda look like a human."

Great Post-Card Art

with Sister Mary Fred

ANTOINE'S

A Famous Restaurant for Over a Hundred Years

SISTER MARY FRED:

Welcome to another episode of Great Post-Card Art with me, your *host*, (*giggle*) Sister Mary Fred. Let's get started, shall we?

All right, let's take a look at our first work of art. As the title card indicates, this post-card was handed out to the patrons of Antoine's, deep in the dark, dank, pulsating rhythms of the nether regions otherwise known as The Big Easy, (*giggle*) N'Ahlins.

What is the true story behind this painting? The real question is: what happened right before this image was captured? As you notice, all eyes are turned in the direction of the two men. Clearly, the woman in pink, her head slightly cocked, doesn't quite know what to make of the spectacle. Although she has raised her glass, she has not committed to this gesture. The woman behind her has obviously pushed her chair back, in hopes of eluding the artist's brush. Is she merely embarrassed? Or, has a dirty little secret been made public? Notice, she has not raised her glass. Her husband, on the contrary, is quite enthused. Aroused, one might rightfully ask?

Behind the two men, we have certainly caught an illicit tryst. We can decipher this by the fact that she has been given her lovely bouquet of flowers at Antoine's and not at home. This, the artist reinforces, by having the gentleman behind them glaring at her, and not the two men locked in embrace.

Which brings us to the focal point of our post-card. Our two men, locked arm in arm. Let us suppose that the gentleman with the glasses is our host. Our *maitre'd*. One can only suppose that the other gentleman with the bottle in hand is our *sommelier*. Notice, if you will, that the *maitre'd* has spread his little finger, so as to gently caress the other's sleeve. Clearly, these two men are in love. So much so, that perhaps, for one brief moment, they can no longer deny it. Look how they peer into each other's eyes.

On closer examination, we see that the *maitre'd* is bending over slightly, while the *sommelier* is thrusting his pelvic region forward. Clearly, he is the pitcher, our host, the catcher. There's a certain kind of poetic symmetry to this Great Work of Post-Card Art.

9

(missing)

Our next masterpiece is from the *Poste-Carte* movement of the early twenties, in Paris. Again, working in a medium of b&w photography, French photographer, Doisneau (or "Doinny" to his friends, among whom, he had none, for "Doinny" was something of a… Peeping Tom, if you will.) He may have been a pervert, but he was a perv with a penchant for photography.

In this shot, Doisneau points his camera through the rear window of a famous brothel in Paris. Famous, as you can plainly see – unless you're too busy unbuckling or unbuttoning various items of clothing! (*giggle*) – this particular brothel specialized in celebrity look-alike whores.

Notice how Doisneau and his camera are super-imposed over the face of the hooker dressed as Josephine Baker, the image of her banana skirt encircling Doisneau's hips, his tri-pod rising both majestically and symbolically between them! Thrusting illusion against reality! Reflection against infection! Truly awe-inspiring with its raw, natives-gone-wild, sexual energy. In this case, the window is a metaphor for a rubber between Josephine's banana belt and Doisneau's… aperture. Oh! (*Sister Mary Fred fans herself with tonight's program*)

One is flushed and exhilarated by the thought of Doisneau running home through the cobblestone streets of Paris, racing up those rickety old stairs, clutching his prize negative under his coat. "*Oh, mais oui!*" Once again, Doisneau has eluded the *gendarmerie*. One can only suppose that later that night, he excused himself from dinner, retired to the master study where he poured himself a fine cognac, sipping with one hand and, er, well, admiring his *poste-carte* with the other. (*giggle*)

Join us next week, won't you? Okay, cut! Who's got the post-card? Lenny? Get your butt over here pronto!

MASTERS & JOHNSON

(The Untold Story)

Although everyone knows the so-called "official" story of Masters & Johnson, very few people have ever heard the untold story. For, simply put, the untold story has never been told. Until now.

On January 15, 1957, Dr. William Masters placed the following ad in the St. Louis Dispatch:

> **WANTED: SWM sex therapist seeks**
> **SWF sex therapist for research.** *(Honest!)*

Although it could have raised an eyebrow or two, in 1957, no one had a clue what SWF meant. The bulk of his responses were guesses. Sniveling, Whiney Frenchmen narrowly edging out Self-absorbed, Wisecracking Filipinos. In fact, by mistake, Masters almost bought a Small, Web-toed Ferret. The transaction was thwarted when the owner insisted on seeing the Sacred Winged Monkey.

As notated in Dr. Virginia Johnson's locked diary (labeled: *Private – Don't Read!*) trouble with Masters began almost immediately:

January 23rd

"It should be Johnson & Masters," I point out to the Great Doctor.
"Why?" he retorts.
"Well," I stammer submissively, "because Johnson comes before Masters."
"Yes, but only alphabetically," he shoots back in total domination.

"Oh," I respond.
His forceful determination is a definite turn-on! (Mustn't let on!)

Try: wearing glasses.

Lose: bullet bra.

Although their "work" together seems to progress well, Johnson apparently cannot let go of the billing dispute. Just prior to placing a large order for personalized stationary, again she broaches the subject.

"It just doesn't sound right," replies Dr. Masters. "Go ahead, try it. Ring-ring. Ring-ring. Ring-ring. Go ahead. Answer it. Ring-ring."

"Answer it, Doctor?"

"The phone. Answer the phone. Ring-ring. Ring-ring."

"Hello?"

"Hello. Who is this?"

"Oh, right. Johnson & Masters, may I help you?"

"Who?! Never heard of 'em! Who is this?! What number did I call?!"

13

"I see your point."

"Good. Hang up. We've got work to do."

The turning point in their illustrious collaboration came at what some might decry a fortuitous moment. Rather than becoming the laughing stock of the entire medical – (*Wait a minute, that's the phone. Hello? ...Yes... Well, Mr. Smarty-pants, as it just so happens, I'm in the midst of writing it now... Excuse me? ...No, off hand, I would not guess it was a turnip truck, no. Although, you do appear to have fallen off something -- could've been a speeding vegetable truck, who am I to argue? ...Not the point?! Well, need I remind you I am not the one who brought up your misfortunate, disfiguring accident... Uh-huh... Well, you know, I'm just sort of fleshing-out the whole thing right now and... Uh-huh... I see. Okay. Right. Good-bye.*)

Well, I'm glad you were present for that little... exchange. The editors have just informed me that if I tell you any more of "The Untold Story of Masters & Johnson" they'll have to change the title. And they call me lazy!

So, join us next time for another Untold Story.

WEENIE & BUN

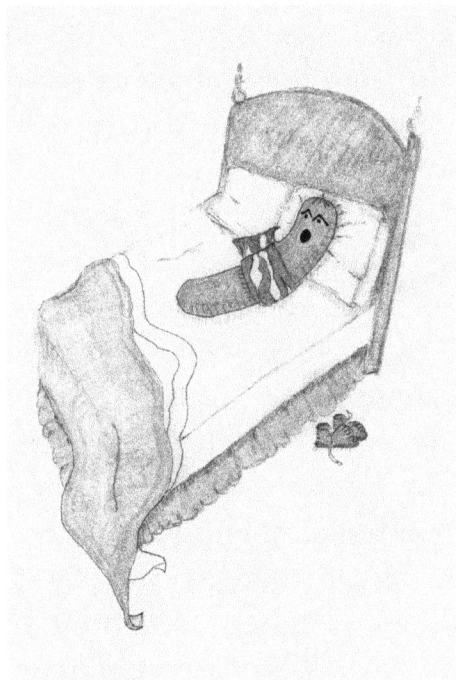

"Weenie! How could you?!"

"For Want of a Sombrero"

(or "The Piñata Incident")

Benny was an ordinary, run-of-the-mill kid. In this case, the mill was a sawmill and his running was seriously curtailed when Benny lost four toes from his left foot. Benny worshipped his Uncle Jack. It was his Uncle Jack who broke Benny of the habit of storing his chewing gum in his ear while eating his lunch.

"No good can possibly come from this," Uncle Jack would admonish.

"What?" Benny would shout, "I can't hear a word you're saying!"

Benny dreamed of playing the cello. "Why can't I have normal dreams like anyone else?" he'd ask. "Like being onstage, naked, forgetting my lines? Or giving birth to a two-headed mongoose? I don't even like cello music. It's a nightmare!"

Benny was born Doctor Benjamin Spillman, his mother was taking no chances. No, Benny would not turn out like his brother, Retired Rear Admiral Fred Spillman.

"Never worked a day in his life! He's a bum!" Mrs. Spillman exclaimed. "Hey, Retired! Get your little rear admiral in here this instant!"

It wasn't easy growing up in the shadow of his elder brother, for Retired Rear Admiral was a dwarf. At noon, with the sun directly overhead, Benny would have to dress his brother in a sombrero and hoist him onto his shoulders just to create a large enough shadow to fit under. It was Cinqo de Mayo, 1987, that Retired Rear Admiral's dream of riding a unicycle blindfolded on the high-wire came to a tragic finale. Unable to find his sombrero, Benny tied the blindfold and stuck a piñata on his brother's head. Retired Rear Admiral's final words were, "Benny! Look at all the candy! Ouch!"

Although Benny ate the candy with the rest of the children, he couldn't help wondering why God made the giraffe's knees bend in the opposite direction and what a giraffe's chair might look like.

In an odd turn of events, Benny was arrested in Italy in 1937 for being pro-pasti.

"Putz!" his father is reported as saying. "Anyone with half a brain in his head is anti-pasti! Everyone but my Benny! Besides, what is it his business? Why doesn't he learn to keep his big mouth shut?!"

While out riding one day, Benny suffered a tragic accident when he was thrown from his seahorse and drowned. Doctor Benjamin Spillman died broke and penniless. "That's redundant!" he gurgled with his final breath. (Unfortunately, Benny was under water and his dying words were misinterpreted as something else altogether.)

17

Said Mr. Spillman at the funeral service, "Benny was an odd bird. Which explains the little piles of speckled eggs we'd find in the corner behind the fichus tree."

Mrs. Spillman, ever the optimist, learned a valuable lesson from the tragic fate of her two boys. "No more screwin' around," she told the assembled mourners, "The next kid we're naming Generalissimo Myron Spillman!"

Truer Than Fiction

The average dog eats three times as many hot dogs as the average Eskimo eats Eskimo Pies.

If the Chinese were lined up head to toe in a mobius strip they would reach infinity.

Elephants never forget, but they do tend to exaggerate.

Milton Berle had the biggest schlong in showbiz, his wife had the biggest smile.

Miniature poodles use the sniff test to determine when to change their outfits.

The breasts of prehistoric men also produced milk. In fact, men's breasts were quite large, weighing nearly twice as much as the modern woman's, and causing them to stoop severely. As the breasts grew smaller, man stood more and more erect. Scientists are currently designing a new evolutionary diagram suitable for ten year-old boys.

"Jungle Bunnies!"

Commentary

Cartoonist Andrew Taylor came under fire recently from a surprisingly vocal minority over his controversial new comic strip, "Jungle Bunnies!" Rabbits everywhere are up in...feet over their depiction.

"Satire?" pondered the Rev. Jumpy Jackson. "Satire can backfire if the car goes too far. In other words, parody is hilarity if it's laughter you're after.

What I'm trying to say is, meaning's like a beaning. It can hit you in the head, and then you're dead. Or rather, social revolution is like prostitution. If with a dime, you buy a rhyme. In other words –"

"Is it me?" asks cartoonist Taylor, "Or is that rabbit nuts? In other words, is that wabbit kwazy?!"

A spokeswoman for the RDL (Rabbit Defense League) had this to say, "You can roast us, boil us and tell us we're no different from chicken – but where are the scary native chickens with bones through their… beaks? It's all about projecting positive role models. The San Diego Chargers have the Big Chicken, where's the Big Bunny?"

"She absolutely right," said Jumpy Jackson. "We live in a land where parity is a rarity. When the Fighting Rabbits change the nation's habits; when we have the Chicago Hares and no one cares; when we have the Georgia Bunnies and all those Southern Honeys; when the —"

"I beg you," begged cartoonist Taylor, "talk to somebody else – anybody!"

Fellow cartoonist, the Danish artist Droog Vlurmann, had this to say, "Praise Allah! I have been praying for this day to come! Finally, they can hang another cartoonist in effigy and I can get on with my life! I don't know what Andy Taylor was smoking, but – "

"Okay," interrupted Mr. Taylor, "not that guy, either. Who else've you got?"

Charlie Brown, beloved cartoon icon, also weighed in, "Does satire really work? I don't know. I'm more of a physical comedian myself. You know, I try to kick the ball, you pull it away, I fall down. Big yuks. I wasn't trying to change the world. If I could've gotten Pig-Pen to take a bath, I would've been happy! You know, you can't change the world, but you can change your socks. That's my motto."

"That's asinine," says cartoonist Andrew Taylor. "Change your socks? You're asking this guy if satire is effective? Seriously, everybody should just chill-out. I recommend you save your energy for my next cartoon, *"Li'l African-American Sambo!"*

"That Thing He Did"

Old Dogs, New Tricks: A Cautionary Tale

He came downstairs and poured himself a bowl of Raisin Bran, just like he did every morning. He pulled out the drawer and grabbed his spoon before adding the milk. Timing. It was all in the timing. The perfect milk to cereal ratio, and timing. Soggy bran didn't just signal the end of his breakfast, it was an indicator for the entire day. He grabbed his spoon and dug in for his first bite.

"Last night?" she said, an eyebrow arched strategically.

He chewed quickly; seeking the necessary consistency to speak without choking.

"It was great, wasn't it?" he said, hoping to avoid any and all further conversation. And, for a while, it seemed to work. Until...

"What'd you do – see a movie?"

"What?" he said with a mouthful.

"Last night?"

"Right," he said, sensing the potential for soggy cereal.

"What are you telling me? You were... inspired?"

"What is this? What're all these questions? You didn't seem to have any questions last night. Suddenly, it's The Inquisition!"

"The Inquisition?"

"Okay, the Gestapo. Is that better?"

"No, I'm just curious, that's all. After fifteen years of marriage, you were suddenly... inspired?"

"What is this? Do you wish to file a complaint? Is that it?"

"No! Don't get me wrong, it's wonderful. It's thrilling to think that every fifteen years you might actually pick up a new move. I'm just wondering, you know, where it came from, that's all."

"Oh, I see. Like I'm completely incapable of coming up with a move all my own."

"I didn't say that."

"Oh, didn't you? *Really?* You didn't?"

He took a bite of cereal… soggy! He set it down as though making a profound statement. He looked up at her; nothing. No response. Ruined Raisin Bran, a proven barometer for the day that lay ahead, and she was not going to give him a response. She knew how bad he wanted it and she refused. There will be no response! A bowlful of Raisin Bran was destined for the garbage disposal and she refused to bend an inch. Let'r rip! Fire up the disposal! I'm ready!

"Oh hell, what have I done?" she thought on her way to work. "He's got that little trick in the bag, that's all that matters. Right? Why question how it got there? Important thing is, it's there… Why make him self-conscious? Last thing in the world we need is for him to feel self-conscious… Oh hell, he will now! Of course he will! Right when he goes to do it, he'll remember what I said. Why wouldn't he? I would. I *will!* When he does it again – *if* he does it again – all I will be thinking about is The Inquisition. Knowing he'll be thinking about it, too… I'll never be able to enjoy it again! I waited fifteen years for the perfect move – what have I done?!"

Lost in thought, she was stunned to find herself pulling into her space in the parking garage. She was obsessed now. Consumed with that thing he did. That thing he did with such… perfection. Such precision. How? Where did he learn it? She got out of the car and headed for the elevators. On the way up, alone in the elevator car, she worked herself into a complete dither! By the time she reached her floor, that thing he did had ended his marriage.

Soggy Raisin Bran, he should have seen it coming…

"OUT OF THE BOX"

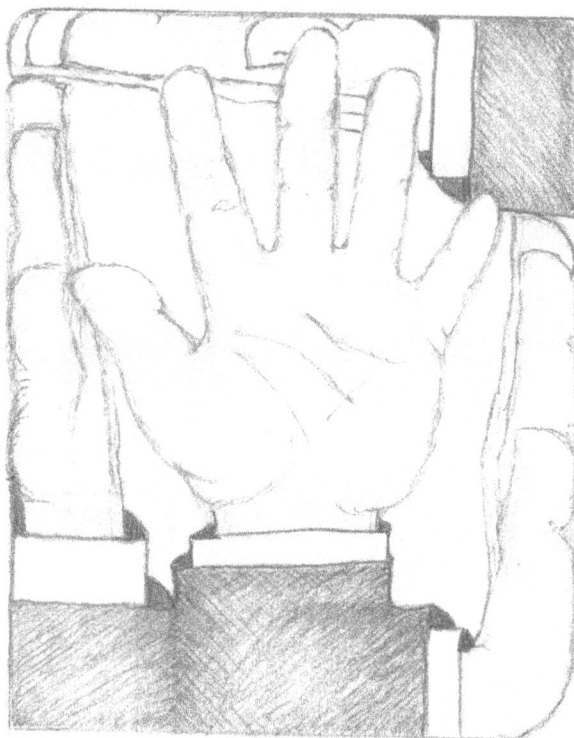

The Autobiography of Marcel Marceau

"   !" ~ *New York Times*

Chapter One

TWO

THE LAST OF THE MOE HOWARDS

The inspirational true story of one man's quest to keep his family together, no matter how fat, bald or stupid.

"Doink!" – LA Times

"Chocked full of n'yuck, n'yuck, n'yucks!" – NY Times

"It'll 'moydah' ya!" – Daily News

Great Post-Card Art
With Sister Mary Fred

SISTER MARY FRED:

This piece is titled, *"Parisian Delight."* We can safely assume our leading lady is, indeed, French. Who else would wear those shoes with that sexy little Parisian negligee? An Iranian? Hardly!

The obvious question raised by this masterpiece of overstatement is, *which* is the delight? After all, both subjects are, presumably, Parisian. So, putting it delicately, is the pig there *to* the delight of our Parisian trollop? Or *for* her delight? Or is it the other way around?

Our painted hussy is clearly trying to convince him to do something, perhaps to perform some act that, for whatever reason, the pig is unwilling to perform. She's on her knees pleading.

"What more do you want?" she implores. "Lipstick, pearls, a little lacey thing cut up to my ass – look at these shoes! I've never begged for it in my life. Look at me. I could get any guy. But I don't want any guy, I want you."

The pig, his tail neatly curled, stands his ground. Or, in this case, his pillow.

"What exactly is this Parisian Delight?" he asks. "Hey, wait a minute. What's that in your hand?"

"Nothing. See?"

"No, the other hand. What's in it? An apple?"

Has "Uncredited," the name of this famous photographer, skillfully captured the Biblical image of Woman (Eve) tempting Man (the pig) into a night of rapturous, toe-curling sin? A night of... *Parisian Delight?* (*giggle*) I like to think so!

Until next week, this is Sister Mary Fred reminding you that Great Art is everywhere, and at post-card rates!

The Lost Testament

The Gospel

According to St. Murray

*O*kay, so, you know, I don't know how these things are supposed to begin, what with all the numbers and colons and, you know, more numbers. But I'm guessing this is 01:01. Or more precisely, for all you guys in the end-zone with your signs at the point-after-touchdown kick, MURRAY 01:01.

MURRAY 01:02

What am I doing here? How did this happen? If I were to tell you that it was a miracle, I would not be exaggerating. If turning the water into wine was His (capital "H") first miracle, then I would be his second.

Imagine if you will, you're working the lunch shift at Carnegie Deli. You know, you're serving orders, bussing tables, chatting it up with the regulars. But all the while you've got your eye on Allison Adams. Tall, long honey-blonde hair. Easily the most beautiful waitress in any deli anywhere.

Allison… the last thing I remember, we were in the cooler, I was on my knee, a small box holding a gold ring in my sweaty little palm.

"Allison," I said, as she reached for a five gallon tub of mayonnaise, "I – "

That's it. Next thing I know, I'm surrounded by a bunch of guys in robes. They're all staring at me and applauding.

"Bravo!"

"What the…?" I looked around at the festivities -- some kinda wedding ceremony or something.

"Encore!" yells this bearded guy, wine glass in hand. "Show us another trick!"

"Later, Peter. There'll be much more to come."

Oh great, a second show. That was my first thought. And then it all sank in… "Oh my God!" I exclaimed.

"Yes?" replied the man with the long brown hair and powder blue robe.

"This is uh, this is the story where your Mother –"

"Mary."

"Right."

"Do you know Mom?"

"The story's starting to come back to me. Mary, The Blessed Virgin."

"The Blessed Virgin? Mom?"

"Oh yeah, right, they don't refer to her as the Blessed Virgin just yet."

"What are you talking about?"

36

"Never mind, it's crazy. I could never explain it. It's just, you know, I'm trying to remember the whole story."

"The story?"

"Yeah, you know, from the book."

"There's a book?"

"The Bible. Jesus! – excuse me – you've never heard of The Bible? It's only the largest selling book ever written. This story – the wedding ceremony – it's in that book. Your mom, Mary, tells you they've run out of wine, so you do a little hocus-pocus and turn the water into wine. Then, I'm guessing, you followed up that little trick by zapping me back in time."

MURRAY 01:03

I explain to Jesus how I need to get back to my real life. He displayed some metaphysical gymnastics to convince me that this is real life. Whatever. Bottom line, I'm still here. Since I seem to know the story, Jesus has asked me to sorta blog the whole thing. Imbedded, if you will, with Jesus and the gang. He swears no one will even know I'm missing. He says He means that in the nicest way, but I don't like the way He winked at Peter.

I met Mary Magdalene today. I told her that somehow I had gotten her story mixed up with the one about the prostitute. Which reminded me of this old joke.

37

"So, you weren't there, but Jesus steps up to all these people with their stones and he says, Let he who is without sin cast the first stone. Right? And this old lady steps up and lets one fly. Jesus turns to her and says, Mother!"

Mary didn't see the humor. Clearly, that's because she's got a thing for Jesus.

"Trust me, you don't want to get involved with Jesus, he's not your type."

"You keep saying that. What do you mean not my type?"

"You know, he's uh, he's a guy's guy. You ever see him with another woman? Never. A lamb now and then, sure. Maybe a donkey on special occasions – Easter, Palm Sunday – whatever. The point is, Mary, I think I'm falling in love with you."

"You?"

"Yes, me. Why? What's so funny? It's the robe, right? I know I'm not much to look at in what – 31 AD? – But believe me, back in my time, in The Village, I was doin' alright."

"The Village?"

"Where I'm from. I told you all this."

"Oh, right. The future."

MURRAY 01:04

Convinced I know the story already, Jesus has asked me to help write his little speeches. Oh well, this will give me an opportunity to win Mary's heart. Things, however, are not going quite as well as I had hoped with Jesus.

"Blessed is the mook?"

"That's meek. Meek. Blessed are the meek."

"Your handwriting is deplorable."

"Jesus, this isn't easy. I'm just trying to fill in the blanks here. Blessed are the..."

"Tall?"

"Are they? Maybe you're right. What do they inherit?"

"Hmm. The tall?"

"Maybe it isn't the tall. Maybe they get squat, after all, they've got height."

"Good point."

"We're going about this all wrong. Let's start with what they inherit and then figure out who they are."

"Okay."

"Like, for instance, who would inherit a toupee? A bald guy."

"Blessed are the bald?"

"Jeez, I hope this caterer comes through. Where's Mary? I heard the roads are all blocked. They're expecting 500 people! What've we got? Five loaves and a couple fish?"

"How do you like this title? Sermon on the Hill."

"I don't like it. Try mount."

"Mount on the Hill?"

"No, Sermon on the Mount."

"Sermon on the Mount. Murray, you're a savior!"

MURRAY 01:05

Somehow, the three fish and five loaves were enough to feed the 500 fans. (I don't know if it was a miracle or Philip's cooking!)

Later that day, with Jesus up on the mount, preaching to all the people, I seized my opportunity. I took Mary aside and told her exactly how I felt.

"I love you. I'm in love with you. I've been in love with you since the first time I heard your name. Mary Magdalene."

"You heard my name? Where?"

"I told you all this – I know it sounds crazy, but there's movies and books."

"Yes, I know. *Your* book. I'm so proud of you, Murray."

"Well..."

"Jesus tells me –"

"Jesus..."

"Why don't you like Him?"

"I like Him. What's not to like? He's great. He's practically perfect–"

"Practically?"

"I tellya, Mary, you're spinning your wheels with this guy."

"Spinning my wheels? This is that machine you keep talking about. I'd love to try the one with no roof! A red one! My veil flowing in the wind!"

"Will you forget about the car for a minute? I'm trying to tell you that I love you."

Just then, this fat guy gets right up between us. "Any more fish?" he says to me.

"No! Can't you see we're busy here?"

"I thought it was all-you-can-eat."

"It is. That's all you can eat. Now am-scray."

As he walks off, I look over at Mary. She has that quizzical look on her face that she seems to get every time we speak.

"Am-scray?"

"It's a, uh, form of Latin."

"Really? You've got so much to teach me."

"Yes, and so little time. It's what – 32 A.D.ish?"

Mary laughed in a way Jesus could never make her laugh. I was sure of it.

"You're so funny!"

MURRAY 01:06

I may have consumed a tad too much wine with supper tonight and said a few things I shouldn't have. At one point, Jesus gets all serious, stands up and raises his wine glass. So, I join him, thinking it was some kinda toast or something.

"This is the blood of my body."

"Jeez," I say, "you keep talking like that and this really will be the Last Supper!"

Big laughs from the boys, except for old stone-faced Matthew, of course. So, right after this, He breaks off a chunk of bread and says, "This is my body."

So, I says, "Well, someone better tell Peter, his hands are all over it!"

Again, big yuks from the fellas. I look over, see Mary getting hit-on at the bar, and decide to rescue her. We talk about dinner, you know, movies and television. She's fascinated with the future.

"Tell me again. How did you get here?"

"There's not much to tell, really. One minute I'm in a deli in New York, thousands of miles and thousands of years away, and the next thing I know – poof! – I'm here."

Lazarus, seated at the next stool, leans over and says, "Big deal. You were in a deli? One minute I'm in the afterlife. I'm in paradise! I'm in a pool with seventy-two topless virgins, when – poof!"

"Seventy-two? How do you know they were all virgins?"

"Oh, you can tell."

This old guy passing by, he stops and chimes in, "Jesus gave me the gift of eyesight."

"Yeah," I says, "So, why are you complaining?"

"Have you seen my wife?!"

Lazarus, the old guy, and me – we all bust a gut over this one. I look over and see that Mary isn't laughing.

"Mary, what is it?"

"I'm going to tell Him how I feel."

"Not tonight."

"But I must. I love Him."

"Yes, I know, but I'm telling you, tonight is not a good night. He's, He's psychic or something."

"Psychic?"

"He thinks someone is going to betray Him with a kiss."

43

"What?"

"I remember something about this part. But it wasn't exactly my... testament."

"Your what?"

"He's right. Someone's going to betray Him with a kiss, but it's not going to be you. Not tonight. Not if I can help it."

"Then who?"

"I don't know. Could be that prissy waiter for all I know. Did you see where he seated me? I'm at a folding card table, for chrissakes! I'm not even in the painting! No one will know I was here. No one will ever know my story."

"But your book."

"My book... You know what, I'm going back to the party. Take my advice. I wouldn't say anything tonight. I've got this weird premonition something's not kosher. Judas has been acting very strange."

Murray 01:07

Last night, after supper, we were hanging around in the park. Anyway, I'd had a little too much wine and I'm starting to doze off when the next thing I know the cops are arresting Jesus!

"On what charge?" I call out.

44

"Loitering!" they holler back.

You know, so I'm thinking they'll let Him sleep it off and let Him go in the morning, but no. Unfortunately, He draws that hypochondriac Herod, always washing his hands and using hankies to turn the doorknob – a real fruitcake.

MURRAY 01:08

I run into Mary out by that disgusting puppeteer with his moronic Hasidic puppets. I don't know why she finds them so funny. Seriously, if there is one defect in this otherwise glimpse of The Maker's Hand, it's her sense of humor. I inform her that Jesus was arrested for loitering and she merely laughs. You see what I mean?

"What's that you were saying earlier? There are people in the future who think I give birth to His child?"

"No. I said there's this whacko nutjob who hacks out a cockamamie murder mystery –"

"Yes, but he said we have a child together?"

"Not in the real book."

"Not in *your* book."

"Not in The Bible."

"But Da Vinci –"

"This has nothing to do with the actual Da Vinci –"

"Yes, but there's hope."

"No. There's no hope."

"Unless…"

"Unless?"

"Unless, Murray, your life had a grander purpose than either one of us ever imagined."

"I'm not following you."

"No? Aren't you the one who said, Greater love than this no woman has ever known?"

"Well, I was improvising. I can't be held responsible for everything that spills out."

"Murray, do you love me?"

"Yes, of course. You know I do."

"Then you'll try. Tell me you'll try to save Him."

How ironic, I thought, me save the Savior? Me, Murray Steinberg, save The King of the Jews?

"Unless, Murray, it's true what they say?"

"Why? What do they say?"

"That you're a sniveling, two-faced, coward."

"Who says this?"

"The Apostles."

"Oh."

Mary moved in, toying with the tassel on my robe.

"So?"

"So?"

"Do you love me?"

"What does my tunic tell you?"

She looked down and smiled. But who was I kidding? I couldn't do it now if my life depended on it. I was running out of time and I was never good under pressure. Performance anxiety, that's what my old girlfriend used to call it. *Performance* anxiety? What was I, a trained chimp? Blindfolded in my cute little suit, crossing a high-wire on a unicycle, holding a frilly little parasol? Well, if that's what she wanted, good riddance! Mary watched as my tent collapsed.

"Murray, what's the matter?"

"Truth is, Mary, if I don't go home soon..."

"What? You act like you already know what's going to happen and it isn't good."

"No, maybe not. Maybe you were right. Maybe everything really does happen for a reason. Maybe there is a God. And maybe I've been sent back to alter the course of human history."

"Wow."

"Maybe it's my destiny to save Him."

"Murray, you're really much deeper than I gave you credit."

"Well, thank you."

"Honestly? When I first met you?"

"Yes?"

47

"I took you for something of a shmo."

"And now?"

"I don't know what's come over me."

"Really?"

"Yes. You're so, so inspirational. So... charismatic."

"You think so?"

"The word... messianic springs to mind."

"No."

"Yes. You're omniscient. The way you seem to know everything that's going to happen before it happens."

"You mean, like this?"

I moved in for a kiss but was instantly rebuffed.

"What are you doing?!"

MURRAY 01:09

My plan is to sneak into the Roman guards' tent and steal a uniform. Thomas, always the skeptic, has no confidence in my scheme.

"What is it, Tom? Don't you think I can slip in there unnoticed?"

"I doubt it."

"Come on, don't you think I can dress up as a Roman soldier and make my way in to see Jesus?"

"Oh, that I seriously doubt."

"What are you – the original Doubting Thomas?"

"I doubt it."

And, of course, Peter had to throw in his two cents worth.

"Stealing is wrong."

"Did I say I was *stealing* the guard's uniform? I'm *borrowing* it."

"You're rationalizing."

"How am I rationalizing? I'm going to borrow the uniform to sneak into the -- Okay, you know what, Pete? I don't have time to sit here and debate this with you. I've got to get in there and see Jesus before it's too late."

"Too late for what?"

"Let's just say we're getting to the part of the story I remember."

02:01

Well, you should have seen the look on Jesus' face when my cross was stood up next to His!

"Murray?"

"The Good Thief, they call me."

Jesus laughed for the first time in days. "If you were so good, how'd you get caught?!"

"Very funny."

"I'm sorry, forgive me."

"Yeah, right. Say three "Hail Marys" and call me in the morning."

Suddenly the sky got all dark. There was lightning and thunder; it's raining and everybody's running around with newspapers over their heads – it was crazy! Jesus just turns to me, cool as could be, and smiles.

"Don't worry, Murray. This day thou shalt be in Paradise."

And presto-change-o, I'm back in the walk-in cooler at Carnegie Deli, Allison is up on the ladder getting the mayo, and I'm down on one knee, looking right up her skirt. Paradise! Lotta people don't know this, but Jesus had a wicked sense of humor.

I looked around the cooler, confused for a minute.

"Marry m-m-m... Mary?"

Just as Allison turned, clutching the tub of mayo, I remembered the gold ring in my hand.

"Did you call me Mary?"

I shoved the little box into my pocket and stood.

"Mary? No, of course not. I said, Marry the ketch-up. I've got to marry the ketch-up."

"Oh. Right. Are you okay, Murray? You look a little pale."

02:02

Well, it's been a crazy few days, what with the translation of my Lost Testament. I've been asked by the publisher to add a post-script. I was waiting for divine inspiration, but what the hell?

I finally asked Allison to marry me. Needless to say, it did not go as I had hoped.

"Are you mentally ill?"

"Allison, I love you."

"I read your little Gospel, Murray. Did you honestly think you could hide Mary Magdalene from me?!"

"Oh, come on! That was what – 2,000 years ago. She's dust by now. You're jealous of a handful of dust. That's all she means to me."

"You'll always be comparing me to Mary Magdalene – how could I possibly measure up?"

"Are you kidding? You've got her beat hands down where it really counts. Life. She's got none. Zero. No life. Hasn't had life for – what is it, Tuesday? – the woman's been lifeless for centuries."

Knowing all her weak spots, I moved in close and gently kissed Allison on the neck.

"Yes, but for you it wasn't centuries ago. For you, it was the blink of an eye. One minute you're here

51

marrying the ketch-up, the next minute – poof – sex with a saint!"

"I didn't actually know her in the… biblical sense."

"But you wanted to."

What was I going to say? No, I didn't want to sleep with the most alluring and fascinating woman of the entire First Century A.D.?

"Allison? Come back! Where are you going?"

"I gotta go, Murray. It's time for my shift at the deli."

And with that, she turned and walked away. Turns out, Allison would rather stare at pastrami the rest of her life than my sorry kisser…

There's a parable that Jesus used to tell about a squirrel and his nut. Or was it a camel and his cud? That's what it was, it was a camel and his cud. I remember this distinctly because I said, "Cow."

"Excuse me?"

"I think you meant a cow and his cud. Or in this case, *her* cud."

"No, that doesn't sound right: A cow and his cud."

"*Her* cud."

"What kind of a parable starts out, a cow and her cud?"

"I don't know, it's your little story, not mine. Stick with a camel, what do I care?"

Anyway, I can't really remember how the parable goes, but the gist of it is, if you've got cud, chew it. If not, uh, you know, don't.

Well, I hope these divinely inspired words have helped to shed a little light. As for me, I know this will sound sacrilegious to some, but meeting Jesus was the single worst experience of my life. And I'll tell Him the next time I see Him, you know, seated at the right hand of the Big Guy. (Not, I might add, a Christian!)

Well, I've got to turn in now, I've got Letterman tomorrow and I promised a few minutes with Pope What-His-Name. And Mother Theresa thought she had it tough with the lepers! Darn you, Jesus!

AMEN.

"When Pigs Fly!"

Flying Pig Baths

"THE COLLABORATION"

Chapter One

"This story will write itself."

"Write itself? What're you talking about?"

"We've got a great ending."

"Yeah, but no beginning."

"This."

"*This?*" he asked in italics.

"This is our beginning."

"Talking about our great ending? That's a beginning?"

"No, moron, not *this*. Not this actual sentence I'm saying, no. Don't write this. Just work from the ending backwards to here. This point."

"This."

"Yes … But not what we're saying, just what happened. Tell the story with words."

"Words."

"Right."

"As opposed to what – buffalo?"

"What?"

"What else am I going to use? Words."

"Yes, but not *these* words, that's all I'm saying."

"Okay."

Chapter Two

"Let me see what we've got so far."

"Well, it's rough."

"That's okay, let me see it."

"I'd rather not. Not just yet."

"Okay. What about narration?"

Hmm. Narration. Not a bad idea.

"What are you writing now?"

"Words, remember? We ruled out buffalo."

"What do you think about the narrative style?"

Ah, yes, the narrative style. What do I think?

"Should it be told in the third person?" he asked in all… *what?* Sincerity? No. Earnestness? No, I hate that word, earnestness. No one ever uses that word in real life. Not in earnestness, he wrote. In the third person. Using a fragmented writing style. Answering his question with words.

"Now I'm concerned," he said, staring straight at me; those sad, puppy-dog eyes begging for a response.

"Yes?"

"Yes, what?" he snapped back.

"You're concerned?"

"I think you're right. We've got no beginning."

Chapter Three

"Are you nuts? We're already four or five pages in – we're way past the beginning. We've got to start thinking about a middle."

"A middle?"

"Every good story's got one. I don't know where you've been."

He didn't, either. He had no idea where he'd been. How, he wondered, can you have a beginning and an ending and nothing in the middle?

"Like that," he pointed, "What are you writing?"

"If you'd shut-up for one second comma I might be able to tell you that I may actually be writing the middle right now."

"Right now?"

"Maybe. Depends on how long our story goes."

"Oh."

"We may be done with the middle for all I know."

"Well then, you see? I was right."

"About what?"

"This story is writing itself."

What the hell are you talking about?! That's what he wanted to say. *Can't you see this pen in my hand?! What do you think I'm doing over here? Tanning buffalo hide?!*

"You know," he said, downing the last drop of his pale ale, "this is so easy, we should write another one. In fact, we've got a much better story –"

Oh no! he thought. *A tangent! Another storyline? A "B" story? A sub-plot? Will we ever be able to connect the two stories? Will it devour our "A" story? Should he be stopped now, before it's too late? Before another tale weaves itself into the texture of our story?*

"Yes, but what about our great ending?"

"I'm starting to think it can't carry a whole story."

"Not even a whole short story?"

"I hate short stories," he said in all earnestness.

The End

The Adventures of
The Madonna & Child

(Inspired by Glenfiddich and characters created by Bob Graham)

"Very funny, Jesus. Now change your brother back this instant!"

" DON'T MISS IT! "

*"Makes you want to light your hair on fire
and jump on the bed!"*

The By-Poehler Review
With Byron Poehler

Today's topic of review: The Times of the Day.
Morning, noon and night. Easy enough. Morning – hate
it! Not much to say on this subject as I rarely roll out of
bed before noon. Which brings us, inevitably, to lunch.
Lunch is good. Who doesn't like lunch? Except
astronauts, I suppose. But how do they know it's lunch?
How do they know that tube of dehydrated wieners and
beans isn't brunch?

Which brings us to that dead horse I like to beat
called "dunch," the meal between lunch and dinner.
Believe me, I completely comprehend why we don't have

"linner" and "lupper," but can someone please tell me what the hell is wrong with "dunch"? Dunch and a dance. 'I'm telling you, Dotty, they simply have the best dunch buffet in town!'

In Hollywood it might not work. I forgot, they don't eat a meal in Hollywood, they take it. Who's going to want to take a dunch? I don't care if it's Spielberg, I'm not taking a dunch with him! Forget I said anything, let's stick with lunch. Whew! This topic is far more challenging than I ever imagined!

After lunch, in the warmer climates – like Spain – they take siestas. The whole family – one bed! It's all hot and steamy and sticky and the sheets are filthy. Somewhere in the distance, a pig oinks. Chances are, they had *frijoles* – let's face it, people – the unvarnished truth, whatever the hell that means. Don't ask me, I detest all that sanding and varnishing and spilling the paint everywhere and you're up on a ladder, brush in one hand, gin & tonic in the other, you're standing on the top rung with the warning that says Don't Stand Here, but they know everybody does. Hell, the guy who engraved the words into the metal stands right on top of them every day! But I'm off on a tangent. On the top rung of a tangent. Why do they call it a rung? Did it ring? Is it a phone? Come on, people! Who's naming these things?!

I know I shouldn't let it upset me this way. My friends all say, "By, are you self-regulating your meds again?" Regulating? Why do I take such umbrage at that word? What does umbrage mean? I'm such an idiot! Wait a minute… Umbrage. Yeah, that's right. You're damn right I feel umbrage!

Okay, now I've really lost the plot, haven't I? Why do I do this? *A self-employed critic?* What was I thinking? Dad was right. Not about the homosexual part, about not amounting to squat – Oh, siestas! That's right, naptime. Naptime? Maybe we shouldn't go there. That sounds like an emotional landmine ready to blow, doesn't it? You know, you're all vulnerable. You're in your undies, curled-up in a fetal position. You're on the floor with all the rest of the – *homosexual?!* Now I really am taking umbrage! I can only imagine how much umbrage I'd be taking if I actually was homosexual. They probably take more umbrage than anyone!

What all this has to do with siestas, I have no idea. Unless they take siestas in Umbria. Ah, to feel the umbrage under an umbrella in Umbria once again… And then to take a long siesta, but, you know, not with a whole family in one bed. Or in the case of Umbria, two lousy beds pushed together to make one big lousy bed, the flies buzzing in and out because God-forbid they should have a window screen!

The By Poehler Review:

Siestas & Taking a "Dunch" with Spielberg:

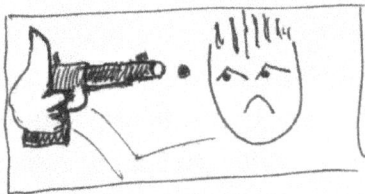

Jewel Records
TRANSCRIPT
"Lost Soles Blues"

by "Blind" Willy McCann

DATE RECORDED: April 6, 1937
PERFORMERS:
"Blind" Willy McCann – vocals; piano
The Herbal Inspirations – vocals

BLIND WILLY:
WOKE UP THIS MORNIN'
COULD NOT FIND MY SHOES
WOKE UP THIS MORNIN', BABY
COULD NOT FIND MY SHOES
HAD TO WALK OUT BAREFOOT, DARLIN'
JUST TO GET THE NEWS

CALLED THE BOSS
SAID I CAN'T COME IN TODAY
I CALLED THE BOSSMAN, PEOPLE
SAID I CAN'T COME IN TODAY
GONNA SOUND A LITTLE CRAZY
BUT MY SHOES HAVE GONE ASTRAY

THE HERBAL INSPIRATIONS:
THOSE SHOES...

BLIND WILLY:
AIN'T GOT THOSE SHOES

THE HERBAL INSPIRATIONS:
THOSE SHOES...

BLIND WILLY:
CAN'T FIND MY SHOES

THE HERBAL INSPIRATIONS:
THOSE SHOES…

BLIND WILLY:
'NUFF TO DRIVE A MAN TO DRINK, BUT…

TOGETHER:
NO SHIRT, NO SHOES, NO BOOZE!

BLIND WILLY:
YOU KNOW I TOLD THE BOSS
BUT HE WAS NOT AMUSED
I SAID, I PHONED THE BOSS
THE BOSS WAS NOT AMUSED
HE SAID, WILLY, GET YOUR BUTT IN HERE
TO HELL WITH YOUR GODDAM SHOES!

I WENT DOWNTOWN, SWEET MAMA
IN MY STOCKIN' FEET!
YOU KNOW I RODE THE SUBWAY, DARLIN'
IN MY STOCKIN' FEET!
WISH I HAD THEM SHOES
SOMETHIN' WET BENEATH MY SEAT!

THE HERBAL INSPIRATIONS:
THOSE SHOES…

BLIND WILLY:
THEM OL' WORN-OUT SHOES

THE HERBAL INSPIRATIONS:
THOSE SHOES…

BLIND WILLY:
THOSE OL' BROKED-IN SHOES

THE HERBAL INSPIRATIONS:
THOSE SHOES…

BLIND WILLY
'NUFF TO DRIVE A MAN TO DRINK, BUT…

TOGETHER:
NO SHIRT, NO SHOES, NO BOOZE!

BLIND WILLY:
YOU KNOW, CHILDREN
I CAN'T REMEMBER WHEN I HAD 'EM ON

THE HERBAL INSPIRATIONS:
THOSE SHOES…

BLIND WILLY:
LORD, YOU KNOW, PEOPLE
I CAN'T REMEMBER WHEN I HAD 'EM ON

THE HERBAL INSPIRATIONS:
THOSE SHOES…

BLIND WILLY:
LOOKED DOWN AT MY FEET, SWEET JESUS
SAW BOTH MY SHOES WERE GONE!

THE HERBAL INSPIRATIONS:
THOSE SHOES…

BLIND WILLY:
LORD, WHERE'D I PUT—

THE HERBAL INSPIRATIONS:
THOSE SHOES…

BLIND WILLY:
IT DON'T MAKE NO SENSE—

THE HERBAL INSPIRATIONS:
THOSE SHOES…

BLIND WILLY:
I WOKE UP AND —

THE HERBAL INSPIRATIONS:
THOSE SHOES —

BLIND WILLY:
WERE GONE!

THE HERBAL INSPIRATIONS:
THOSE SHOES…

BLIND WILLY:
I DIDN'T KNOW WHAT TO DO

THE HERBAL INSPIRATIONS:
THOSE SHOES…

BLIND WILLY:
I MEAN, I HAVE TO HAVE --

THE HERBAL INSPIRATIONS:
THOSE SHOES…

BLIND WILLY:
WHAT I'M TRYING TO SAY IS –

THE HERBAL INSPIRATIONS:
THOSE SHOES...

BLIND WILLY:
IF I COULD GET A WORD IN EDGEWISE --

THE HERBAL INSPIRATIONS:
THOSE SHOES...

BLIND WILLY:
UH, LADIES? I'M TRYIN' TO TELL THE PEOPLE 'BOUT

THE HERBAL INSPIRATIONS:
THOSE SHOES...

BLIND WILLY:
YOU KNOW, IF I HAD ME --

THE HERBAL INSPIRATIONS:
THOSE SHOES...

BLIND WILLY:
I'D WALK RIGHT OVER AND KICK YOUR FINE LITTLE

THE HERBAL INSPIRATIONS:
THOSE SHOES...

BLIND WILLY:
'NUFF TO DRIVE A MAN TO DRINK! BUT...

TOGETHER:
NO SHIRT, NO SHOES, NO BOOZE!

BLIND WILLY
IT'S TRUE, PEOPLE! I GOTS TO FIND

THE HERBAL INSPIRATIONS:
THOSE SHOES…

BLIND WILLY:
THEM OL' HIGH-STEPPIN' SNEAKERS

THE HERBAL INSPIRATIONS:
THOSE SHOES…

"Sunset on the Brow"

A collection from the High Life of The Low Brows

"Okay, who forgot to replace the toilette paper?"

The reviews are in for "Sunset on the Brow"

**"Finally someone has given voice to the fears and dreams
of the tiny creatures inhabiting our eyebrows.
Bravo & Eeeuuuwww!"**

**~ Byron Poehler ~
The By-Poehler Review**

Mr. Ed
The Final Days

The Scene: Mr. Ed is in a hospital bed at The Old Animal Actors Hospital, a buxom blonde Nurse at his side. Mr. Ed is "feeling his oats," flirting with his nurse.

WILBUR'S VOICE: Ay-hem.

The Nurse looks over.

NURSE: Oh, I see you have a visitor.
MR. ED: A visitor? *(he looks over)* Oh, no.

Wilbur steps up to the bed, a small bouquet of wilting flowers in hand.

WILBUR: Hello, Mr. Ed.
MR. ED: Weeelburrrrrrr!
WILBUR: Well, you don't sound too thrilled to see me.

Mr. Ed watches as the Nurse swings her hips out of the room.

MR. ED: As always, your timing is peccable.
WILBUR: I believe the word is *im*peccable.
MR. ED: You also believe Gilligan is stranded on that tiny island.
WILBUR: Not the *real* Gilligan!
MR. ED: There is no *real* Gilligan, you moron!
WILBUR: Look, I didn't come here to have this same old argument.
MR. ED: Fine, we'll start a new one. Sit down. Make yourself at home. Take off your shoes, stink up the joint. What the hell do I care?
WILBUR: Oh now, Mr. Ed, what's gotten into you?
MR. ED: A whole lotta oats. And I can tell you what's coming out, too, if you're so damned interested.
WILBUR: Here, look, I brought you some flowers.

MR. Ed: Great, are they edible? The food in this hellhole stinks!
WILBUR: ...Edible? Well, I –
MR. ED: It was a joke, numbskull! *(aside)* Well, I see some things haven't changed.

Wilbur sits on the edge of the bed.

WILBUR: You know, I was thinking maybe we could drop the "Mr." and I could just call you Ed.
MR. ED: There you go thinking again. Didn't we learn that lesson in Episode 547 with that enema bag and the Alka-Seltzer?
WILBUR: That wasn't my fault!
MR. ED: Well, don't look at me! I don't have thumbs, remember?
WILBUR: I didn't come here to –
MR. ED: Yeah, why did you come here, anyway?
WILBUR: I haven't seen you this bitter since Francis –
MR. ED: Jackass! I told you never to mention his name!
WILBUR: ...Wait a minute. Did you just call *me* a jackass?!
MR. ED: Well, if the shoe fits!

Wilbur gets up from the bed and sits in the chair.

WILBUR: I didn't realize Francis hurt you so bad.
MR. ED: Well, not as bad as the day you had me gelded, but –
WILBUR: I apologized for that!
MR. ED: Apologized? Is that supposed to cover it? Sorry we cut off your –
WILBUR: Do we have to –
MR. ED: If you say, "beat that dead horse again" I swear I'm going to rip out these tubes, come over there and –
WILBUR: *(standing)* Well, maybe I should go.
MR. ED: Sure, go. Leave your dead flowers and your crummy chocolates and get the hell out!
WILBUR: ...I, uh, I didn't bring chocolates...
MR. ED: You didn't bring chocolates? You're such a Wilbur. You realize that, don't you?

Wilbur slowly backs toward the door.

WILBUR: Listen, *Mister* Ed, I just wanted to stop by, for old time's sake, you know, before your… *operation.*
MR. ED: Operation? Wilbur, I broke an ankle, that's all. It's nothing. A new cast and I'll be trotting out of here, ready to chase the fillies.
WILBUR: …A cast?
MR. ED: What are you hinting at? You want to sign it?
WILBUR: Uh, yeah. Yeah, that's it. I want to sign your cast, Mr. Ed.
MR. ED: You always were a horrible liar.
WILBUR: I guess we learned that in Episode 912 with those two skanky hookers.
MR. ED: Don't remind me, I itched for days!
WILBUR: *(laughing)* Well, me too!
MR. ED: Yes, but you can scratch. Look at me, it was torture! I don't know what I would've done without you.
WILBUR: *(looking off, dramatically)* Ah yes, I remember it well…
MR. ED: You're not going to break into song about scratching my private parts, are you?
WILBUR: Well, you know, I've been doing a lot of dinner theater ever since the show was –
MR. ED: Like me – after I get that cast removed – put out to pasture.
WILBUR: I was going to say, "given the axe," but your way sounds like a much nicer way to, uh, well –
MR. ED: What the hell are you blathering about? You remind me of Donald O'Connor in "Francis Joins the Convent"! You're always mincing around, wringing your hands and whining like a schoolgirl about this or that. I'm starting to wonder exactly who it was they gelded that day. Listen, do me a favor, willya, hand me those flowers on the way out, I'm starving!

Wilbur picks up the bouquet of flowers and hands them to Mr. Ed. He eats them as Wilbur heads for the door. He suddenly turns around and faces Mr. Ed.

WILBUR: Okay, fine! I never mentioned this – for ten years and another however many in syndication – I never once said how pompous I thought it was that you should insist on being called, "Mister"! Who the hell are you, Virgil Tibbs?!

MR. ED: Who?

WILBUR: Never mind, I'm leaving!

MR. ED: Not without a kiss.

WILBUR: What?

MR. ED: I want a kiss.

WILBUR: A kiss?

MR. ED: For old time's sake.

Wilbur approaches, cautiously.

WILBUR: Uh-huh. You're not going to take a bite out of my cheek or anything, are you?

MR. ED: Weelburrrr, don't you trust me?

WILBUR: You? A snide, sarcastic, foul-mouthed equine? You, *Ed?* A talking horse? An utter impossibility?! Do I trust a talking horse, you ask? Need I remind you that I lost everything to Maryanne in that settlement agreement? Everything! The house, the stable! Everything! I still can't fathom where anyone got hold of a film of me scratching your private parts to sell on the internet!

MR. ED: All those comparisons to Tommy Lee – it was humiliating!

WILBUR: And what about the lighting? It was horrible! Totally unflattering. Everything was so grainy and out of focus that you could hardly tell –

MR. ED: I hate to interrupt your touching soliloquy, but stick a sock in it, willya? It's time for my 6 o'clock sponge bath.

Wilbur follows Mr. Ed's gaze to the door and the buxom blonde Nurse.

WILBUR: Uh yes, well, I better run along.

MR. ED: Oh, Wilbur. One last thing before you go.

WILBUR: Yes, Mr. Ed? Is there something you wanted to tell me?

MR. ED: Yes. See if you can't rustle up a copy of that DVD and high-tail it on back here, pronto. Comprendo?

WILBUR: I comprendo, Mr. Ed. I comprendo.

Wilbur shakes his head in disgust as the Nurse approaches the bedside.

WILBUR: Good luck with that… *operation.*

As Wilbur turns and exits the room, we hear a GUNSHOT…

FADE OUT

THREE

The Low Brows

SUNSET ON THE BROW

Sunset on the Brow

The Low Brows

Okay, who forgot to replace the toilette paper?

The Low Brows

ATTACK

OF THE...

EYE-BROW PENCIL!

The Low Brows

Stand-up Comedians

"Crazy Lenny"

"So, this amoeba flagellates into a bore hole and says, 'I'll take a dozen eggs!' But seriously folks, I just crawled in from the nose so I've got to warn you, tonight's material's 'naughty! You get it? Snotty! What are you – a bunch of single cells?!"

The Low Brows

Coming Soon!

TWEEZER!

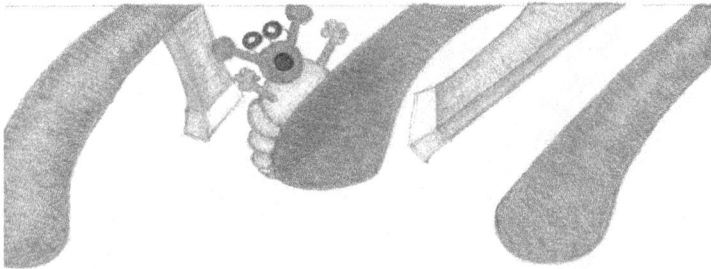

Deleted Bible Stories

So, Lot says to me, 'Don't look back whatever you do.' 'Why,' I says. 'Why?' he snaps at me, 'Have you seen Sara?' 'Sara? No. Why?' I ask. 'She's turned into a statue of salt!' he says. 'Salt?' I say, 'This I gotta see!' Next thing you know, I'm Peanut Man.

Why do I think my story was deleted? Well, it's who you know. Connections. See, if I were an Apostle or Jesus' Uncle Bernie or something, damn right you'd know my story.

Kids in Sunday school would've loved to color me. Instead, what they get is Sara – a pillar of salt! White! Try coloring salt when you're three and a half!

Call me a conspiracy nut, but it all comes down to that Apostle Thomas. When Lot says to me, 'Tom, don't look back! Sara's turned to salt!' you think I believed him? No, of course not! Would you?! I'm the original 'Doubting Thomas,' but what would that Apostle have, if not the "Doubting" moniker? He's like one of the Seven Dwarves you couldn't name. Did he sneeze? No. Hmm. Did he whine? (Was Whiney one of the Dwarves or the Apostles? I always get that one mixed up.) Anyway, I doubted Lot first. It's the Old Testament – look it up.

Sodom and Gomorrah? It was like Minneapolis and St. Paul. Sure, Minneapolis stinks, but St. Paul? Should St. Paul be destroyed? It didn't make sense. It was, frankly, a senseless God we had to deal with in the Old Testament. Wrathful. Like turning people into salt or peanuts – for what? Turning around?!

All the things in the world, He chooses to appear as a burning bush. Not just a bush, mind you, but a burning bush! He could've come as a puppy or a bunny or something cute. Of course, our God would've made it a burning bunny, so maybe it's a good thing it was a bush.

A pyracantha comes to mind, what with all those thorns and all? I hate pyracanthas! Hell, I'd burn one if I had one. That doesn't make me God. Oops! I hope that wasn't blasphemous! I've got enough trouble as it is – look at me. I'm The Peanut Man. I could've been Doubting Tom!

Anyway, like I was saying, I can see why you might not like Sodom – especially in the summer, with all the crowds. Personally, I think it was a P.R. problem waiting to happen. I was there the day they were coming up with names for the town. Believe it or not, St. Paul was almost the name. Then some wiseacre stands up and says, 'St. Paul? Who the hell is that? This is the Old Testament!'

Did I mention our God was smiteful? Gomorrah is a perfect example of the way our God worked. We're a suburb; a bedroom community, right? You don't like San Francisco values, you don't destroy Burlingame. So, me and a bunch a people in Gomorrah, we're like, 'No way. God is just. He's like a bee. He only stings--' So, Lenny interrupts and says, 'Oh yeah? I got stung once and I wasn't doin' nothin'.' Hmm, I hmmed to myself, Lenny might be right.

Just then, my brother Lot comes running by us – I mean fast! He's with Sara and the whole family. 'Lot,' I yell to him, 'Where you off to in such a hurry?' 'Who was that?' Sara asks him.

Lot says, 'Forget about it. It's nobody. Don't look back!' 'But…' she says. The rest of the story, as they say, is history. Or at least, *Biblical.* She's salt and, instead of Doubting Tom, I'm The Peanut Man.

"Holstein vs. O'Looney"

The Great Debate

When Kathleen O'Looney married Clayton Holstein, she, like so many women of her generation, chose not to take his last name.

"A cow?" asked Kathleen. "Katy the Cow? Is that who I am? I don't think so."

"Well," said Clayton, "I'd rather be Clayton the Cow than Coo-Coo Clay, The Nutcase Boy."

Kathleen insists she tried to hammer-out a compromise. "I added the 'O' at his mother's insistenc –"

"*Request.*"

"Well, she *requested* it insistently and incessantly. Anyway, apparently that wasn't enough for Clayton the Cow."

"I see. *O'Nutcase* is so much better than just plain Nutcase. 'Right this way, Mr. *O'Nutcase*. By all means, Mr. *O'Nutcase*. Anything you want, Mr. –"

"*Okay*, we get it!"

"I still think my solution makes a whole lot more sense," said Clayton, defiantly.

"A hyphen?" Kathleen shot back.

"Why not?"

"O'Looney-Holstein?"

"Why not?"

"The Crazy-Cow? How is that better? It's not! It's like saying you've got the flu. Do you want vomiting or diarrhea? *Both?* Well, okay, it's your choice."

Kathleen stared at Clayton, awaiting a return lobby – anything. Clayton just glared at her in stony silence.

"What?" she asked. "Didn't that make sense? It was an analogy or a metaphor or whatever. I'm just saying –"

"You're saying what, Kathleen? Exactly who am I in your little analogy? Diarrhea?"

"No. I didn't say that."

"Oh. Well, maybe I missed the point in your graphic little metaphor or whatever it was. Are you saying 'Holstein' is like vomit or—"

"Let me try another analogy. Suppose your name is 'Piles' – 'Gomer Piles' and my name is 'Hillary Hemor—"

"Where the hell did that narrator go?"

"In your opinion, the best solution for your daughter is to be introduced as Sarah Piles-Hemorrhoid."

"I never said that!"

"No, you're right. You and your mother would be quite content to have her introduced as Sarah Piles-O'Hemorroid!"

"Cow-O'Nutcase! I mean, Holstein-O'Looney!"

"You're right, where the hell is that narrator? He comes in here and stirs up that old debate and then hides on some other page. Well, I'm sticking around till page three, just to see if that little weasel has the little weasel balls to actually finish this piece! …Why are you laughing?"

"Little weasel balls."

"Yeah, Weasel Balls. Good name for him!"

"Weasel Balls O'Nutcase."

"Well, looky here. Page three."

Yes, Clayton and Kathleen did, indeed, carry this ridiculous debate all the way to page three. An old wound had been opened, conflict – the essence of drama – had been established and I, the humble narrator, have reappeared for the final paragraph, to deliver the perfect tag-line. For what is in a name? Would not a cow, by any other name, smell as –"

"The perfect tag-line? I don't think so. I don't think you can do it."

Although I had clearly written: the final paragraph, Kathleen O'Looney is apparently illiterate. Would not a cow –

"Hey, Weasel Balls, can you read *this?!*"

The O'Loonies, being a proud people –

"Yeah, too proud to change their names!"

"I added an 'O'!"

As the Cow-O'Nutcases begin to repeat themselves, I suggest we bid good-night –

"You see? I knew you couldn't come up with the perfect tag-line!" said Katy the Cow, not knowing when to shut the hell up!

"MEMOIRS"

(working title)

I spent my formative years in the fascinating world of mainland China. My father, an enigmatic character, was a diplomat for the State Department. Although, it never made sense to me, for he didn't speak a word of Chinese. (He could barely speak English, for that matter.) I'll never forget the time he said, "Mary-Lou, that was the best damn chicken salad I ever tasted!" It wouldn't have been so unusual except for the fact that he was yelling at the dog for peeing on the carpet at the time.

(Note to self: Change China to Walla-Walla/chicken salad to rump-roast/dog to pot-belly pig named Rufus)

Great Post-Card Art

with Sister Mary Fred

SISTER MARY FRED:

Our next piece is simply titled, "1951 Donut Queen". The Queen is shown here with runner-up, Princess Glazed, Miss Ohio. (What's got holes coming and going and "hi" in the middle?) As you can see, she is demonstrating the "talent" that won her the coveted title, balancing four plain donuts. Oh my, the competition must've been fierce! What did Miss Ohio do – fill a Bavarian cream? Or was that left to the judges? (*giggle*)

The "uncredited" photographer was subsequently arrested after his bogus beauty pageant.

"Hey," he said, with the police carting him away, "Obviously, it was a joke! Look at the crown – it's cardboard!"

In the landmark trial, The People vs. The Donut Queen Contest, this photograph was deemed pornographic. Not so much for the scantily dressed Donut Queen, herself, but for the public display of what turned out *not* to be the runner-up, but in actuality, the photographer's life-size sex doll. In fact, in a 5 to 1 decision everything about this post-card was legally declared "whack" material. *(giggle.)*

Until the next time, this is Sister Mary Fred saying, Great Art is everywhere – and at Post Card rates!

"O Brother, Where **Aren't** Thou?"

The Unauthorized Autobiography of...

Chang & Eng

Written without his brother Eng's consent, Chang tells the enigmatic story of the world's first "Siamese" Siamese twins.

Chang takes the reader inside a world that only the truly bored or demented could possibly imagine. From the initial surprise in the delivery room to Chang's eloquent eulogy at Eng's funeral, this book dares to tell the complete story of one man's, uh, two peoples…uh, well, see for yourself as you glimpse inside the pages of this soon to be released epic story.

THE EARLY YEARS:

As fate should have it, the delivery room Doctor's actual words were transcribed verbatim in the patient's chart:

"Congratulations, it's a boy! …And… another boy! Or… No… It's uh… They're a boy! I don't mean to laugh, but, well, frankly, you've got to see this to believe it!"

"Nursing wasn't exactly a picnic," their mother is quoted as saying. "I don't know what we would've done with a third head!"

High school was a particularly hard time for Eng. Although Chang was quarterback and captain of the football team, Eng was relegated to water boy.

From Chang's own personal diary, we gain a unique insight into the brother's complicated relationship and a high school wound that apparently only festered with time:

Eng looked me straight in the eyes. "I couldn't help it!"

"Oh right!" I said. "You didn't have a date to the Homecoming Dance so you didn't care if you had white-heads the size of Mt. Vesuvius!"

"Brother, you sure can beat a dead horse!"

"I can't even look at that prom photo. I keep wondering when your face is going to erupt!"

"It was twenty years ago!"

"I coulda nailed Gloria Pappenfus that night!"

"Okay, Chang, I didn't want to tell you this, but you forced me."

"What?"

"It's about Gloria..."

"Get outta here!"

"It's true."

"My own brother? Eng, how could you?!"

Recent interviews with Gloria Pappenfus, however, paint an entirely different picture:

"Did I love Chang? Yeah, I think so. You know, as much as you can love a guy who's... attached... to another guy. Not attached sexually. That's a whole 'nother chapter! Don't get me started on that story! We'll need another round if we're gonna start talkin' about Donny! ...What? Oh right, Chang and Eng. You know what irked me the most? 'Our' song was 'his' song, too! I know it's a little thing, but with Siamese twins, you'd be surprised how quickly the little things add up.

"If I sound a little bitter, it's because Eng detested 'our' song. He'd mock it, singing it like Maurice Chevalier. I don't care what your favorite song is, if Eng sings it like Maurice Chevalier, you'll never want to hear it again! (*poor imitation*)'Camptown racetrack five miles long. Doo-dah, doo-dah!' You see? Perfectly good song -- Garbage!

"Okay, yeah, maybe I am just a little bitter. I mean, there we were, the Homecoming Dance, Chang and I are King and Queen. The dance floor is empty, a baby blue spotlight shinin' down so dreamy-like. The band starts to play 'our' song. I'm in the arms of the man I love. This should've been the happiest day of my life, right? I open my eyes and who do I see staring at me? Eng! Had his zit exploded at that moment... It's too horrible to imagine!

"Yeah, you're damn right I'm bitter! He's inches from my face, mouthing the words to 'our' song like Maurice Chevalier! Mocking me!

"I still don't know who it was felt me up that night in the back of the Ford. I just remember Eng giggling like a school girl."

College life didn't seem to fare much easier for the boys. The details are a bit sketchy, but apparently Eng was thrown out of school for copying from Chang's exam.

THE SALAD DAYS:

"I really didn't mind stocking the salad bar," Eng is quoted as saying, "but Chang simply refused to help. He mumbled something about *heads* of lettuce and adamantly refused to wash his hands after using the restroom. That's how I got fired. I tried to explain that to the lady down at the unemployment insurance but she couldn't stop laughing long enough to listen. How would she like to lose her job just because her brother refuses to wipe?!"

"Eng?"

"What?!"

FIRST TASTE(S) OF SUCCESS:

After trying their hands at numerous occupations, Chang and Eng found their niche playing professional baseball.

> *It was very difficult for us that first year,* writes Chang, *I played for the Yankees and Eng played for the Mets.*

For the entire season, they were down each other's throats – literally! Eng was so mad when the Yankees won the pennant that he refused to stand for the national anthem, creating quite a spectacle.

The following year they were traded to the Minnesota Twins. Said fellow teammate:

"Whitey, that was my nickname. Which was kinda ironic since we was all whities back then! 'Cept for Chang and Eng, of course. We had to come up with something special just for them. So, we called Eng

'Kitten' – you know, Siamese? …What? A term of endearment? Are you kidding me?! No, you know, when he'd strike out, some of the guys would yell, 'Meow!' I'm talkin' his own teammates!"

Overcoming the obvious obstacles, writes Chang, *we flourished in major league baseball.*

"Flourished?" questions Whitey. "They ended up getting on base a lot, I s'pose. Truth is, they got hit by a lotta fastballs. And I don't think it was on purpose, neither. You know, they were tough to pitch to. Chang was right-handed and Eng was a southpaw. But I mean to tellya, they put on one helluva show! Laugh? They had us all in stitches! You see, Chang was our pitcher and Eng was our catcher – you had to see it to believe it!"

CIRCUS LIFE:

That's where I met my first wife, Florence, writes Chang. *Florence already had the sequined gown and the red balloon. All we needed was a blindfold and a set of steak knives and we had ourselves an act.*

"Oh, I don't blame Chang for my little… mishap," said Florence at the time. "Eng was hitting the bottle pretty heavy back then. I knew when I put that balloon in my teeth. Somehow, I just knew…"

Eng has tried to take her place, writes Chang, *but he looks ridiculous in that sequined gown!*

101

Now, unable to perform their famous act, Chang and Eng were determined to create a new act.

As fate should have it, missing that balloon that day changed all of our lives forever. I suppose you could say it was the greatest day of our lives. Well, maybe not for Florence, but really, what do you need a nose for?

"Easy for you to say," quipped Florence, "you've got two!"

THE BURLESQUE YEARS:

With the success of our new act, The Great Swami Rivers, Eng and I were invited to perform all over the world.

Although the act seems quite lame now, the burlesque crowd had never seen anything like it. Chang, wearing a large turban, would attempt to read Eng's mind.

ENG: Not tonight, I'm not in the mood.
CHANG: Eng?
ENG: I'm warning you. I wouldn't traipse
    around in there if I were you – which I almost am!

(Chang closes his eyes and concentrates. Chang laughs.)

CHANG: You're right, Eng, my mother-in-law sure is fat.

(Chang concentrates; suddenly opens his eyes in shock.)

CHANG: Eng, how dare you?! That's my wife!

(*Eng does a slow burn; looks straight out at the audience, smiles and shakes his head.*)

ENG: I told you not to look!

Curtain.

"I told you not to look!" became one of the biggest catch-phrases of its time, making Chang and Eng the Toast of Broadway.

"GO WEST YOUNG... MEN?"

It didn't take long for Hollywood to take notice. Although their first feature film, the lavish Technicolor musical "TWO BRIDES FOR ONE BROTHERS" bombed miserably at the box-office, Chang & Eng were now bonafide celebrities.

> *At one point we were as big as Abbot & Costello. Bigger! Promoters loved us because we worked for half the price!*

VIVA LAS VEGAS!

With the slow lingering death of burlesque, the boys took their act west.

We took singing lessons, tap dancing lessons, hired a 20-piece band, bought a gold lamé suit and we were ready for Vegas!

With our top-hats and our canes, we'd dance off to a standing ovation every night.

TOGETHER:
BUT WE'LL TRAVEL ALONG
SINGING OUR SONG
SIDE BY SIDE!

It was in Las Vegas, performing three shows a night, seven nights a week, that Chang & Eng fine-tuned their act. Their first real success came with the now-classic routine, "WHO'S *BORN* FIRST?"

CHANG: Eng's been jealous his whole life because my head popped out first.

ENG: (*aside to audience*) I'd like to pop his head out!

ARE TWO HEADS BETTER THAN ONE?

It was in Vegas that I met Lurlene, my second wife. It was on our honeymoon that I first sensed that we might encounter a few obstacles with Eng:

ENG: I won't listen, I promise. Is the game on? What time is it? La-la, la-dee-da. You done yet?

104

Lurlene pulls the silk belt from her robe and approaches Eng.

ENG: Don't worry, I won't look.
ME: No, don't!
LURLENE: Relax, Chang.
ENG: Yeah, loosen up.
LURLENE: I'm not going to strangle him, I'm going to tie him up and blindfold him.
ME: But he loves that!

> *I found out much later that Eng harbored a deep seeded resentment, and not just because I didn't name him as my Best Man. This explains why he got drunk at the reception and hit on Lurlene's sister. It was all downhill from there:*

ENG: I feel... I don't know... threatened by her.
ME: That's ridiculous. Why?
ENG: She's always making these subtle hints.
ME: Like what?
ENG: Like leaving those surgical pamphlets around the house—
ME: You're being paranoid.
ENG: Am I? Or am I going to wake up one day in a jar on a shelf after some botched mellon-ectomy?
ME: Have you eaten? How's your blood sugar? You're not thinking straight.
ENG: You laugh, but I'll be the one with the nose pressed to the glass, my eyes wide open, that dopey look on my face and a dusty little plaque: Eng's Head. That's all it will say.

ME: Eng's Head? No. I'm sure it will say something
about your famous Siamese twin, Chang. Maybe there
will be a famous black & white photograph of me staring
at the jar, my nose pressed against yours.
ENG: You say that now, but…

Frank Sinatra, who happened to catch their act on a
magical night, called Chang & Eng "their own little rat
pack." That night, Frank and the sell-out crowd watched
as the lights went down and the boys took the stage
singing:

CHANG:
I'VE GOT YOU!

ENG:
HEY!

CHANG:
UNDER MY SKIN!

ENG:
WHOA!

CHANG:
I'VE GOT YOUR HEART

ENG:
YEAH!

CHANG:
DEEP IN THE HEART OF ME!

From there, they launched into the crowd favorite, "TWO HEADS ARE BETTER THAN ONE."

ENG: Well, sir, you're an expert on the subject, are two heads better than one?

CHANG: That's kind of a personal question.

ENG: Too personal?

CHANG: Yes, I'd say.

ENG: Whether or not you thought two heads were better than one?

CHANG: Yes.

ENG: Oh, I see. Too personal for me. Your brother.

CHANG: Yes.

ENG: Well, that's it then, I can't go on!

CHANG: With the routine?

ENG: No, being your brother!

CHANG: You're serious?

ENG: Yes, I am!

(*Eng looks away.*)

CHANG: But Eng, what would I do without you? How could I go on? There's no way. I couldn't do the act without you, Eng.

ENG: Ah, then two heads <u>are</u> better than one!

(*Chang does a slow burn, looks out at the audience and shrugs their shoulders.*)

The orchestra plays "They Can't Take That Away."

CHANG:
THE WAY YOU BRUSH MY TEETH

ENG:
THE WAY YOU WASH MY FEET

CHANG:
THE WAY YOU BLOW MY NOSE

ENG:
THE WAY YOU CLIP MY TOES

A SURGEON dances onstage with a saw.

TOGETHER:
NO THEY CAN'T TAKE THAT
(point to each other's head)
NO THEY CAN'T TAKE THAT
AWAY FROM ME!

SUCCESS GOES TO THEIR HEADS

In the end, of course, they did take it away – everything.
The cars, the booze, the broads.

Times are lean, but not Eng! Two can live as cheaply as one? Tell that to Eng! He eats like a pig! In fact, he's such a pig, he uses my hands to stuff cocoa-puffs down his own gullet!

It was shortly after this that Eng suffered his first nervous breakdown.

It was sad. At the end, Eng didn't even recognize me. "Oh, hello," he'd say, "New here?"

Oddly enough, Chang lived another two years after Eng's passing.

At first, I refused to lie down in the coffin. I wouldn't do it for anyone else, but Siamese twins have a special… connection. After all, I know he'll be lying there right beside me when it's my turn.

PLACE STAMP HERE

Post-Card Rate Theatre

Post-Card Rate Theatre

"Is he looking at us again?"

"Yes, and he's not wearing underpants!"

"Act like me. Just ignore him."

"I can't! He's staring at my breasts!"

"Wait a minute... how did he take off his underpants?"

"This is so creepy!"

WEENIE & BUN

"Says here I'm part chicken beak..."

"Chicken beak? Eeuuww! Who wrote that? P.E.T.A?"

"...Chicken beak?"

"Don't worry, Weenie, if you're part chicken beak, I'm sure you were a free-range chicken beak."

"Yeah, you're right. Just me and my chicken beak, roamin' the range. Freely. Geez, those damn P.E.T.A. people make it sound so unromantic!"

WEENIE & LITTLE LINK

"A vegetarian?!"

FOUR

Cocktail Party Survivors

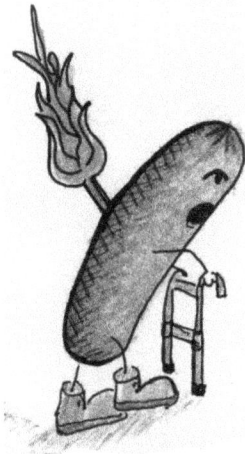

"What do you mean I don't qualify for disability?!
Have you seen this thing sticking out of my back?!
I used to be a swimsuit model!"

The Cocktail Party Players

Present

William Shakespeare's

"To Bean or Not To Bean"

"If you prick us, do we not… juice?"

Cocktail Party Survivors

"I said you had to be twelve to get pierced!"

Cocktail Party Survivors

"The Cocktail Lounge Singer"

The story of a cocktail wiener who dreamed
of following in Frank's footsteps.

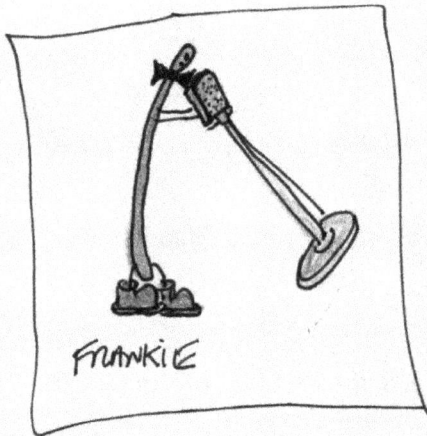

"I'm getting condimental over you."

In lieu of flowers, the family has requested donations be made to the...

MAKE A KVETCH

FOUNDATION

Let an elderly person get it all out before it's too late.

OLD GEEZER:
My son was a putz! A complete imbecile! But did I ever say, "Shlomo, what the hell was that? What were you thinking? Moron!"? No! Never! Once, before I die, I'd like the opportunity to say, "Shlomo, you putz! What the hell were you thinking?!"

Won't you help make a dying man's wish a reality? Please donate to the *Make a Kvetch Foundation* today!

"The Hummingbird Singer"

*The story of a hummingbird
who dreamed of something more… lyrics!*

The Warbler	Albert	Record Producer

Treatment for a Classic 1930's WB cartoon

Featuring the hit song:

That Ain't No
HUMMING-BIRD!
(Jazz Syncopation)

HE'S GOT WORDS!
"HMMM?"
WORDS!
"HMMM?"
HOW CAN HE BE A HUMMINGBIRD?
HE'S GOT WORDS!
"HMMM?"
WORDS!

NOT JUST SCAT
NOT BIZ-BUZ
OR DING-BAT
BUT WORDS!

WHAT KIND OF HUMMINGBIRD'S
GOT WORDS?
"HMMM?"
HE'S GOT WORDS!
"HMMM?"
WORDS!

NOT SCOOBIE-DOOBIE
NOT DOOBIE-DOO
NOT HA-CHA-CHA
OR 23 SKIDOO!

HE'S GOT WORDS!
"HMMM?"

THE BIRD'S GOT WORDS!
"HMMM?"
HE'S NOT JUST WINGIN' IT
THIS BIRD'S SINGIN' IT
HE'S GOT WORDS!

We establish the lives of the HUMMINGBIRD COMMUNITY in the garden, as well as Albert, our lyricist, his Father, Mother, and girlfriend, Cynthia.

ALBERT AT WORK...

Albert plucks the strands of a spider's web making various notes.

> ALBERT:
> *(sings)*
> HMM-HMM,
> HOW I LOVE YA,
> HOW I LOVE YA,
> MY DEAR OLD HMM-HMM!
>
> Darnit, why can't I get this?!
>
> HMM-HMM,
> I'D FLY A MILLION MILES!
> FOR ONE OF YOUR SMILES!
> MY HMM-HMMM-HMM!

DRAMATIC SCENES WITH AL'S FATHER...

> ALBERT:
> Dad, do that again.

FATHER:
What? This: Hmm-hmm-hmm!

ALBERT:
Yes, that! Hmm-hmm-hmm!
(sings)
NIGHT AND DAY!

FATHER:
Al, son, what're you doing?

ALBERT:
I don't know. It just comes out. Isn't it great?

FATHER:
 No, son, it's not great. That's, that's…
unnatural.

ALBERT:

Why?

FATHER:
Why? Because we're hummingbirds, that's
why! Do you think they call us that because we
forgot the words? Hmm? No! Because we
hum. That's what we do. We hum.

ALBERT:
I guess this is a bad time to ask for singing
lessons?

IN THE GARDEN…

Albert is an embarrassment to his parents.

ALBERT:
(sings)
STICKING MY PROBOSCIS
INSIDE A HIBISCUS
GETTING ME SOME NECTAR
FROM A ROSE NAMED HECTOR

FATHER:
Why can't he just hum like the rest of us?

MOTHER:
Hmmm?

IN THE NEST…

Tensions mount.

ALBERT:
It's a gift, Dad.

FATHER:
A gift?! A sweater is a gift. Hmm? A toaster
oven, that's a gift. A blender, a fondue set,
these are gifts. Hmm? Try taking back a lyric.
Where you gonna go, hmmm? Even with a
receipt! Forget it! You wanna give me a gift,
hmm? Knock off the singing!

Albert realizes he'll have to leave the roost.

ROMANCE…

Cynthia, the hummingbird Al leaves behind…

ALBERT:
But I don't understand, Cynthia. I wrote this for you.

CYNTHIA:
I'm not a singer, I'm a hummer. I can't pretend to be something I'm not. Call me narrow-minded, but that's just the way I am.

ALBERT:
Well, that's just… narrow-minded.

CYNTHIA:
Albert! How dare you call me that!

SYNOPSIS:

Albert leaves the nest for The Big City where he meets a prolific young composer. A Record Producer hears their song and signs them to a contract. A cute young Warbler comes to the recording studio to sing their new song and Albert falls madly in love.

The song is #1 on the radio. Albert and his partner start pumping out the hits. The Warbler continues to sing their songs and discovers fame in nightclubs with her new act.

Back at the nest, the hummingbirds have been following Albert's success. The newspaper announces the wedding engagement of Albert to the Warbler. Cynthia is in tears! Albert's Mother consoles her.

Just when Albert's star couldn't shine any brighter, scandal erupts! Songbirds file suits against them for plagiarism!

As it turns out, Albert's partner was a mockingbird! When he splits with all the birdseed, The Warbler calls off the marriage. Albert returns to the nest, a broke and disillusioned little hummingbird, vowing never to sing again.

                    FATHER:
Albert?

                    ALBERT:
Hmmm?

                    FATHER:
Why so glum?

                    ALBERT:
Hmmm-mmm...

                    FATHER:
Listen to this. It's nothing special. Just a little ditty I've been knocking around. Hmm-hmm Hmm-hmm-hmm-hmm.

                    ALBERT:
Wait, Dad. Do that again.

                    FATHER:
Hmm-hmm hmm-hmm-hmm-hmm.

                    ALBERT:
Hmm-hmm hmm-hmm-hmm.
                    (sings)

BEHIND THE GARDEN WALL
WHEN STARS ARE BRIGHT
YOU ARE IN MY ARMS

Cynthia hears his song and joins in.

CYNTHIA
THE NIGHTINGALE
TELLS HIS FAIRY TALE
OF PARADISE WHERE ROSES GREW

TOGETHER
THOUGH I DREAM IN VAIN
IN MY HEART IT WILL REMAIN

FATHER:
MY HMM-HMM HMM-HMM-HMM

We reprise the song 'That Ain't No Hummingbird!" as we
FADE OUT.

WB

DATE: January 22, 2006
TO: Bernie Weintraub, Paradigm
FROM Jana Fain, VP Creative Development
RE: "The Hummingbird Singer"
Treatment for a Classic 1930's WB Cartoon

Dear Bernie,

You still owe me two crab cakes from the Ivy, not that I was counting. (Remind me never to pee and leave you with the appetizers!)

I think the coverage below adequately sums up our collective feelings (whatever feelings we have left!) regarding this project.

Chow!

Jana Fain
VP, Creative Development
(read but not dictated)

WB

COVERAGE: "The Hummingbird Singer"
WRITER: William J Royce
FORMAT: Treatment for a "Classic" 1930's WB Cartoon

Someone should inform Mr. Royce that it is no longer 1930, and hasn't been for quite some time. Perhaps, under the rock from which the author climbed out, they are still making 1930's "Classic" Cartoons. In which case, maybe he can find his rock and crawl back under it, before it hops into a cucumber taxicab and races away!

Mr. Royce throws all logic out the window, where, he tells us, it bounces right back up thirty floors, flies through the window, careens off the kitchen counter, landing smack dab in the middle of the pancake batter! No doubt, underscored by some snappy little number, also from 1930!

Does Mr. Royce honestly expect us to believe "Stardust" was written by a cloying little hummingbird named Albert?! Maybe we should all crawl under the author's rock and hide from the real world, where cars don't dance the samba, and a tongue sandwich doesn't leap out of the bread and lick your face! Maybe he's right. Maybe we should escape for seven and a half minutes. And then what, Mr. Royce? Do we not return to the same drab little cubicle with an obstructed view of a water tower?

As to the plot (if we can stretch that word to its limits) enough already, we get it! Anyone who's seen "Oz" knows to go home, and stay the hell away from the winged monkeys! (If Mr. Royce is so hell-bent on making a "Classic" Cartoon, maybe he should consider "Winged Monkeys!")

I understand that this is supposed to be a parody of "The Jazz Singer" with Al Jolson -- can't somebody write an original parody? I have yet to read one that isn't based on another source!

RECOMMENDATION:
PASS on "The Hummingbird Singer"
BUY Mr. Royce a calendar

WEENIE & BUN

"Exactly what good are all these seeds?"

"What?"

"Seriously. What are you going to do?
Climb on top of me and deposit your load?"

"What's come over you?"

"I mean, it's not like I'm going to give birth to a litter of
cocktail weenies."

"Bun? Are you toasted?"

"Not yet."

Great Post-Card Art
With Sister Mary Fred

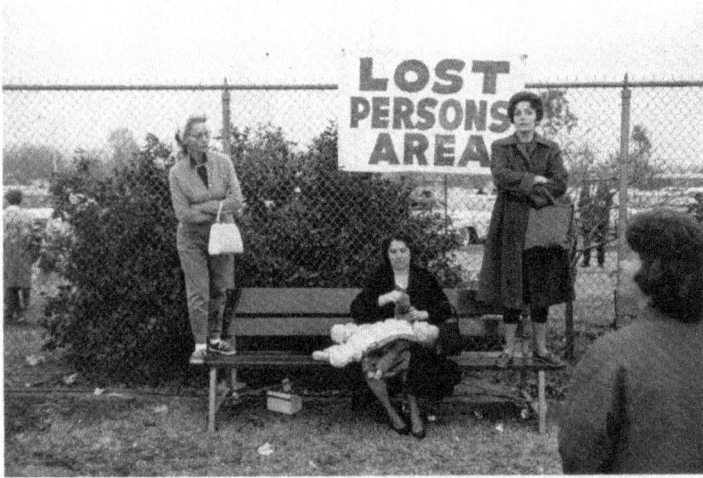

SISTER MARY FRED:
This first piece, "Lost Persons Area," is aptly titled, if
nothing else. Perhaps it is our sign-painter who is lost.
Lost in a foreign world, lost in a foreign language.
Persons? Perhaps he's from a culture – like China –
where they say things like "shrimps." As in, *I'll have an
order of the Sweet & Sour Shrimps, please.* Perhaps, in
his culture, one can have lost "peoples."

      However, let us delve a little closer, shall we? My
second impression upon viewing this Great Work of Post-
Card Art is that what we have here are three lost
persons, a baby, and a spectator, clearly watching the
show from the audience.

      Notice the subtle color choices in handbags – the
black and the white. Clearly, these two women represent
good & evil. They are, simply put, the devil and the
angel. The bench, in this case, representing the
allegorical shoulders from which they perch, locked in
constant battle.

You're quite right to ask if the woman seated in the middle doesn't, perhaps, represent The Madonna, and the child on her lap, the Baby Jesus. Does this poignant photograph ask -- in this permissive society -- if we have "lost" The Madonna and Baby Jesus?

Both visually and grammatically, the artist is trying to tell us that we are not looking at Lost "People" for this is the tableau of a Lost "Persons" – fragmented into the basic components of good/evil, Madonna/whore. But the photographer tells us we are merely a witness to this little drama. We are in the audience – a good seat. Top dollar. No obstructions. No pillar or column or old lady's beehive hairdo, but front row seats to this depressing little black and white spectacle we call life. Bravo!

Ah, but not so fast. For when we flip this post-card over, we see that it says: *Pasadena – 1963*. So, how lost are we really? We have a date and a place, what more do we need? What are we? Some slouch who can't hold a hand or keep eye contact with our caregivers? We're so lost that we have to stand on a bench to be seen in a crowd of three?

Or maybe we've missed the artist's intention altogether. For this is Pasadena. Home of the Rose Parade, a New Year's Day tradition. Notice that the photographer, Elliott Erwitt -- an alias if I ever heard one. (Unless he worked with Lois Lane and Clark Kent. *Hello, I'm Elliott Erwitt.* Somehow, I just don't think so!) Anyway, notice that Elliott places a box under the bench. Is this not an *homage* to Hitchcock's bomb under the bus seat? The very definition, if you will, of... suspense!

"Where are we?! I'm lost! Lost with all these other persons! Lost beneath the sign of incompetence!"

Our photographer has the audacity to paraphrase Shakespeare. "Life," he tells us, "is a sign painted by some illiterate foreigner." Not quite as eloquent, Elliott Erwitt, but you've made your point.

In the battle of good versus evil, Elliott Erwitt shows us in no uncertain terms that in 1963, evil had a strong foothold. For, indeed, our angel with the white purse is giving ground to the devil; she is literally slipping off the allegorical shoulder.

"Go ahead," she is saying, "Don't breastfeed. Give Baby Jesus stewed carrots and peas. Look at that bitch, you fight her! I'm outta here! I missed the whole damn Rose Parade! Besides, there's a box under this bench and it's giving me the willies!"

Which brings us neatly back to Hitchcock's bomb beneath the bus seat. In this case, the McGuffin appears to be a box from Winchell's Donuts. Nevertheless, the suspense is tangible! Is society about to "lose" these "persons"? Are we witnessing the fragmented individual in 1963, before their innocence is obliterated by all that is lurking in that little pink box? Are we *déjà vu*-ing the crucifixion of Kennedy and the redemption by The Beatles? Which, conveniently, brings us back to Lady Madonna. Coo-coo-ka-joo.

Until next time, this is Sister Mary Fred reminding you that Great Art is everywhere -- at post-card rates!

(Place Stamp Here)

Professor Buddy's Post-Card History

Professor Buddy's "Post-Card History"

ART UNLIMITED AMSTERDAM
POSTBUS 1760 1000 BT AMSTERDAM TEL: 020-6851011

Is it any wonder this post-card was published in Amsterdam? The center painted face is quoted as saying, "Ooooh!" This was, no doubt, in response to where he was being held.

Although entitled, "Best Face Forward," this is actually the cover photo for the never released album, "Abbey Train Track." This fictional band went on to die posthumously, prompting the rumor, "Lemon is dead." Prompting the inevitable response, "Who?"

"Abbey Train Track" would have been a seminal album for the band, featuring the premonistic track, "Here Comes the Train!"

HERE COMES THE TRAIN
TOOTIN' TOOT-TOOT
LITTLE DARLIN',
LOOKS LIKE IT'S COMIN'
AWFULLY FAST!

LITTLE DARLIN',
WE BETTER HAUL OURSELVES
SOME ASS!
HERE COMES THE TRAIN!
TOOTIN' TOOT-TOOT

Not to be outdone, Lemon wrote one of his most popular
unreleased songs to date.

HERE COME OI' SMOKESTACK
HE COME STEAMIN' UP QUICKLY
HE GOT
ANGER GROWIN'
HE GOT
FINGER SHOWIN'

HE GOT STEAM BLOWIN'
FROM THE KETTLE
GOT THE PEDAL TO THE METAL
AND HE'S HEADIN' FOR ME!
SQUISHED TOGETHER
RIGHT NOW
ON TRACK THREE

Tragically, the band was killed recording what would
have been their last song for the album, ironically
entitled, "The End."

> AND IN THE END
> THE TRAIN YOU SMASH
> IS EQUAL TO
> THE TRAIN YOU CRASH

Prophetic, if not poetic, I suppose. Oh well, until the next
time, this is Professor Buddy saying, Smoke 'em if you
got 'em. And, if you do, see me after class for some extra
credit.

Weenie & Bun

"You're right. I don't know what I'll find out there.
But life with you is too predictable!

BEST LAID PLANS

Leo was drawn to her like a bad analogy to a desperate writer. She puckered her lips as if to say, "Come and get it, Tiger." Unfortunately, not being much of a lip-reader, Leo misread her pucker and handed her a mackerel. Which, of course, she took the wrong way (under her arm) and left in a huff. (A two-door huff with tinted windows.) Leo would've felt remorse, but having never felt "morse" he believed it was impossible.

Leo was a complex man. He'd sit for hours and contemplate the great questions of the Universe: The meaning of life and what a phone would look like if our ears were attached to our asses. However, the thing that perplexed him most was chicken-fried steak. He couldn't comprehend how the chickens held the spatula. Or for that matter, where they found tiny chef hats to fit them.

This obsession would prove to be his downfall. On impulse one day, Leo bought himself a chicken and worked with her for months. He planned to start her out with fish sticks, next Salisbury steak, gradually bringing her up to the ultimate... filet mignon. And as fate should have it, in this chicken, Leo discovered a purpose in life.

"To teach a chicken to fry a steak," he would say with a tear in his eye, "is everything!" Unfortunately, after months of training, all she was able to cook was spaghetti with clam sauce.

The fact that Leo was a bachelor living with a chicken became the topic of conversation among his neighbors. Still, they had to admit she made one hell of a spaghetti vongole and could lay three times a week. (Which was more than could be said for most of the wives in the neighborhood.) Nonetheless, Leo felt compelled to explain their relationship to everyone. "We're just good friends," he'd insist.

"Fine," his neighbor would reply, "All I asked for was a cup of sugar."

Then one day, as she was rubbing a steak with a clove of garlic, Leo began to notice how the light played with her feathers... Her cute little upturned beak... He felt an uncontrollable urge to fondle the wattle that dangled from her chin like tiny, sagging red balloons.

Stricken with shame and consumed with guilt, Leo packed his bags and took the first Greyhound to Alaska. Unfortunately, the dog didn't adjust to the extreme weather conditions and refused to pull the sled. Leo realized that Anchorage was not the answer. And he was right, for the question was, "More coffee?"

Leo returned home to find a rump roast, a baked potato, and message scribbled in gravy. "Leo," the note read, "it's no use. I'll never learn to fry a steak. I've left for Paris to study at the Cordon Bleu."

"Some men are born to greatness," he said. "Others achieve it, and others have greatness thrust upon them. And others are deserted by chickens who can't even fry a steak!"

Leo realized this was a ridiculous thing to say and wished he'd never said it.

The Adventures Of

Amy the Amoeba

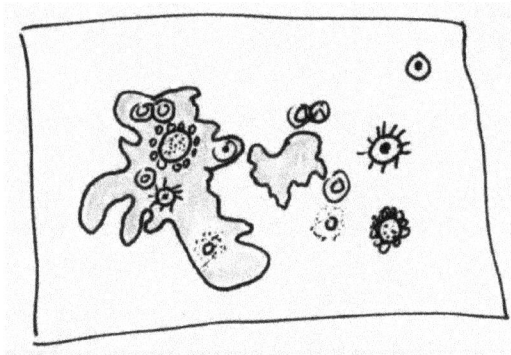

"Sorry. I was never good at division..."

Deleted Monologues

"WHEN PIGS FLY!"

FOUR ONE-ACTS by WILLIAM ROYCE

IN
SHOWCASE
AT
THEATRE EXCHANGE
11855 HART STREET
N. HOLLYWOOD, CA.
SEPTEMBER 15, 16, 17
EIGHT O'CLOCK P.M.

ADMIT 2

From One-Act Plays

"TRIANGLE"

At precisely 8:00, while the houselights are still on and the audience is finding their seats, NANCY, 30's, rearranges all the furniture for the set of the living room. She is completely unaware of the audience. At 8:07, when the set is exactly as it was when Nancy began rearranging the furniture and the audience is nearly seated, Nancy crosses Down Center, back to the audience, and admires her work. Perfect! Houselights Fade Out. Stage Lights Fade Out.

In the darkness we hear...

NANCY'S VOICE: That's right, acupuncture.

The stage lights come on to reveal Nancy seated at the yellow Formica kitchen table. She is speaking on an "old fashioned" phone with a long, yellow, curled cord stretching to a wall Off Stage Left.

NANCY: Anyway, he comes home after his appointment
       and tells me that his semen is toxic to his body....
       Right. No, "Hello, how are you? What's to eat?"
       just, "My semen is toxic."....Well, I know, Joyce,
       that's what I'm thinking!....(Laughs hysterically)
       No, of course not, I couldn't tell him that!....No, so
       anyway, he tells me that his energy wanes with the
       moon and --....His energy. Oh, wane....It's not a
       who, Joyce. Wane, to wane, had waned --....Well,
       I'm getting to that, if you'll let me finish. This
       could be why no one's ever told you. It means,
       when the moon gets smaller, that's all.... Okay,
       next time I'll just say that....Fine.

NANCY: So, he comes home and – Oh, get this. I have toxins, too. That's right. You wouldn't know it to look at me....Well, thank you, Joyce, I never thought so, either. And here's the bad news, you've got 'em, too....Mm-hmm. But don't take it too hard, because we're the lucky one....That's right. We get to have a menstrual cycle to wash them out....That's right. Turn the dial to Menstrual Cycle with a gentle spin and then hang us out to dry. That's our lucky little -- Oh yes, of course, because – and this is the truly sad part. Ready? Men – you remember them, the unlucky ones? – the only way they can rid themselves of their toxins? You guessed it!....Uh-huh, isn't that terrible?.... Yeah-yeah.....Acupuncture. It's a science as old as prostitution and almost as expensive! Mm-hmm. Well, that's what I said. I said, "Chuck, what do I look like – a leech? I'm not exactly jumping at the opportunity to suck the toxins out of your body!"

Off Right we hear the sound of a car pulling into the driveway and smashing into a tricycle.

NANCY: Uh-oh, gotta go. Captain Toxic has arrived.

Nancy crosses Left, following the long yellow phone cord Off Stage as Chuck, mid-thirties, enters, Stage Right.

Great Post-Card Art
With Sister Mary Fred

SISTER MARY FRED: Welcome to a very special
edition. We're so excited! For Pledge Break, we've
taken the show live to the exciting Blues Capitol of the
World, Memphis, Tennessee! Let's take a look at our
first piece this evening, shall we?

"The Peabody Memphis," this great work of Post-Card Art proclaims, *"The South's Grand Hotel has been home to the world-famous Peabody ducks for over 60 years."* Well, by all means, if it's good enough for the ducks! Hard to beat that recommendation in Tennessee, I suppose, unless it's the place where the squirrels lived for over 70 years! Interesting to note that the ducks are world-famous, not the hotel.

"Hunh? Where? Oh. You mean the one with the world-famous ducks? Yeah, okay. What you wanna do is hang yerself a U-ie 'n head back towards the Waffle House."

The South's Grand Hotel. Yep, there's only one and this is it. Look no further, after all, these ducks didn't!

Follow me inside this majestic hotel – *watch your step!* – for we have a special guest tonight, the former assistant manager, Arthur Flemming. I understand you were witness to an historic event?

FLEMMING: Oh Good Lord, yes. I was here workin' the desk that day. I'll never forget it – sixty years ago next Tuesday. This duck walks up and asks for his key. I looks over at Vern, he's flabbergasted. "Your key?" I says to the duck. "What's the name?" I'm thinkin' fast, you know. There's not a duck born can out-think Ol' Flemball Flemming, no sirree! But wouldn't ya know it? Fast as Jimmy cracks corn this duck says, "Miller." "Miller, hunh? Well, we'll just see about that." And what do you know? He's registered, all right. A penthouse suite!

I tap the bell, but the duck places a wing over my hand and says, "That won't be necessary." I look – there's what? – five of 'em and no luggage. I look a little closer and I see it's one mallard and four hens! But hey, you know, to each his own – and three more! Shoot, if I could get four, I'd be right there with 'em in that fountain!

149

SISTER MARY FRED: Well, thank you very much for that... colorful little anecdote, I'm sure the donations are pouring in. Now, if we –

FLEMMING: Then, 'bout a year later, Ray Charles steps up to the desk and says to me, "Sir," he says, "Do you have the temerity to stand there and tell me you'll rent a room to a duck, but I can't stay at this hotel?" "Temerity?" I says, "What's that? Some kinda sauce? Like teriyaki? 'Cause we don't have that, neither. So, off hand, I'd have to say we don't have temerity. But those ducks sure are cute, aren't they? Have you seen 'em waddle off the elevator together?"

SISTER MARY FRED: Yes, how... quaint. Let's see, maybe there's someone else we can speak to? Oh, yes. Hello. We can see by your nametag that you are Mr. Sonny Rhodes and that you are a maintenance engineer. I suppose, in your position, you must have an opinion on your little web-footed friends.

SONNY: Yeah, they make one helluva mess! But it's great for the flowers. Just take a *gander,* I always say.

SISTER MARY FRED: Oh dear, that's a goose.

SONNY: What's that? A goose? No, Sister, I don't know where the geese stay. Sorry!

SISTER MARY FRED: As I mentioned, we're coming to you live from Memphis – and so are most of the people! Well, let's take a *gander* at our post-card of the world-famous ducks, shall we? Our tiny cherubs appear to be setting a qualifying time on the bucking catfish while holding up a world of duck... enhanced flowers. Yee-ha! Until next time -- believe me, there'll be no next time – this is Sister Mary Fred saying, get me out of here!

150

Pick Your Own Caption with…

Weenie & Bun

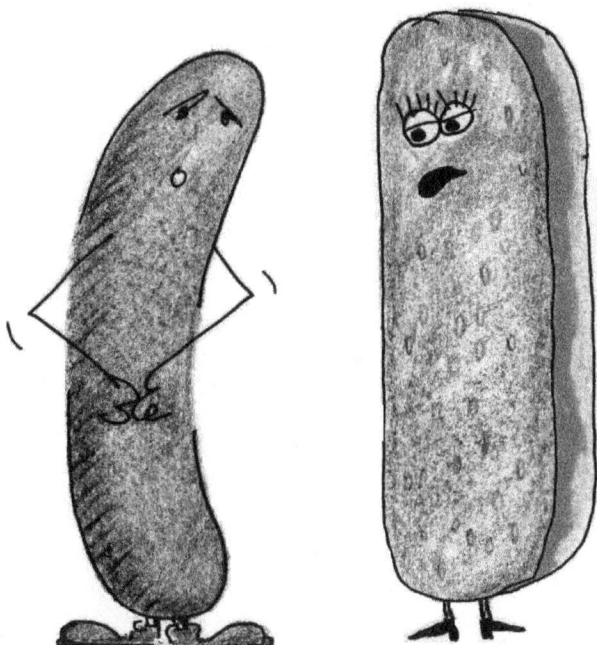

"*Der Weiner <u>Fizzle</u>!*"
"*Don't worry. More than a bunfull is wasted.*"
"*I just asked for a cocktail – don't take it personal!*"
"*Foot-long? Yeah, if it's a rabbit's foot!*"
"*Well, I see why they call you 'Teenie' Weenie.*"
"*I thought you said you were Kosher?*"
"*Not the kind that plumps when you cook 'em, eh?*"
"*I heard you were mostly filler. Guess they forgot to fill that part!*"
"*Boy, when they said meatless wiener, they meant it!*"
"*Are you happy to see me or is that a human in your pocket?!*"

DEDICATION

When I learned that my oldest friend, Jim Whearty, had ALS, I asked what I could do to help. "Write," was Jim's response. "Make me laugh." This book is an attempt to repay my friend for a lifetime of laughter.

www.ingramcontent.com/pod-product-compliance
Lightning Source LLC
Chambersburg PA
CBHW031959040426
42448CB00006B/426

* 9 780615 750439 *